MACMILLAN R
INTERMEDIAT

EZEKIEL MPHAHLELE

Down Second Avenue

Retold by F H Cornish

MACMILLAN

Founding Editor: John Milne

The Macmillan Readers provide a choice of enjoyable reading materials for learners of English. The series is published at six levels – Starter, Beginner, Elementary, Pre-intermediate, Intermediate and Upper.

Level Control
Information, structure and vocabulary are controlled to suit the students' ability at each level.

The number of words at each level:

Starter	about 300 basic words
Beginner	about 600 basic words
Elementary	about 1100 basic words
Pre-intermediate	about 1400 basic words
Intermediate	about 1600 basic words
Upper	about 2200 basic words

Vocabulary
Some difficult words and phrases in this book are important for understanding the story. Some of these words are explained in the story, some are shown in the pictures, and others are marked with a number like this: ...[3]. Phrases are marked with [P]. Words with a number are explained in the *Glossary* at the end of the book and phrases are explained on the *Useful Phrases* page.

Answer Keys
Answer Keys for the *Points for Understanding* and *Exercises* sections can be found at www.macmillanenglish.com/readers.

Contents

A Note About The Author

The black African author, Ezekiel Mphahlele was born on 17th December 1919. He was born in a poor suburb[1] of Pretoria, South Africa. His family were members of the Sotho tribe. Ezekiel is a name from the Bible. Biblical names were often given to children from Christian families – Ezekiel's father was called Moses. Ezekiel was often called 'Eseki' by his family when he was young, but as an adult, he preferred the name 'Es'kia' because it sounded more African.

Between the ages of five and thirteen, Ezekiel lived with his grandmother – his father's mother – in north-eastern Transvaal (this area is now called Limpopo Province). His brother and sister went with him and they all lived in the country. Their parents stayed in Pretoria, where they were unhappy together as Moses was violent and often drunk.

The standard of education where Ezekiel lived in the country was not very high. When he returned to Pretoria, at the age of thirteen, his new teachers said he was 'backward[2]'. But he soon started to do well at school and became good at the English and Afrikaans languages, as well as his native Sotho language.

Soon Moses was on trial for beating[3] Ezekiel's mother and he left the family home forever. Ezekiel and his mother, brother and sister went to live with his other grandmother – his mother's mother – on Second Avenue, in the poor black suburb of Marabastad.

Childhood was difficult for Ezekiel like it usually was for black children in South Africa at that time. But he loved English and all school subjects except mathematics and he worked hard. After he left primary school in Marabastad, he went to a good boarding school in Johannesburg. He later spent two years studying to be a teacher at a training college in Natal (now called Kwa-Zulu Natal).

Ezekiel then discovered that he could write stories. His first book of short stories, *Man Must Live*, was published in 1946, a year after he married Rebecca Mochedibane. Ezekiel hoped to spend a peaceful life teaching and writing, but there were political changes in South Africa which made this impossible. After protesting against new education laws, he was arrested and he spent a short time in prison. He was soon freed, but he was banned from teaching in South Africa. He worked as a journalist for a while, but in 1957 he left South Africa with his wife and three children to teach in Nigeria.

For the next twenty years, Ezekiel stayed away from South Africa. He taught in different universities – mostly in the USA. He had got BA (Bachelor of Arts) and MA (Master of Arts) degrees in South Africa and in 1968 he got a PhD (Doctor of Philosophy) in the USA.

He also spent time in France and several African countries. Then in 1977, at the age of fifty-seven, he returned to South Africa to live.

In 1994, Ezekiel, who was sometimes called 'Uncle Zeke', was awarded the Order of the Southern Cross – South Africa's highest honour – by Nelson Mandela*. Ezekiel died on 27th October 2008.

Ezekiel Mphahlele wrote several autobiographical books including *Down Second Avenue* (1959) and *Afrika My Music* (1984). He also wrote a major book of literary criticism called *The African Image*. But most of his books are short stories and novels. *Chirundu* (1979) is his most famous novel.

* *The Macmillan Biography*, Nelson Mandela, *is now available at Pre-intermediate level. See the Macmillan Readers catalogue or visit www.macmillanenglish.com/readers for more information.*

A Note About This Story

This book is an autobiography. In it, Ezekiel Mphahlele tells the story of his life in South Africa from the age of five up to the age of thirty-seven. He writes about his childhood by telling lots of stories about his relations and about people he knew. As a black South African, he soon learns about racial difference and racial prejudice[4].

The country in which Ezekiel grew up was the Union of South Africa. This country was created in 1910. It was an independent country within the British Empire. The rulers of this country were white people whose families had come from Europe – from Britain and from the Netherlands. These white 'settlers' had ruled the different parts of South Africa many years before their areas had joined together in the Union. The people of British background spoke English. The people whose families came from the Netherlands spoke Afrikaans – a local version of the Dutch language. They were called Afrikaners.

These groups of white people had all the political power in the Union, but they were a small minority. The other inhabitants were divided into different 'racial' groups. The Africans were the black people who had always lived in the area, and who spoke several African languages. Many of them spoke one of the European languages too. People called 'Coloured' were of mixed race – mostly people with an African parent and a European one. There were also Asiatic people – people who the Europeans had brought from India and sometimes China to work for them in the nineteenth century. In some parts of the country the Coloureds had the same rights as whites, but in other areas they were badly treated. The Asiatics were treated worse than the Coloureds and the Africans were treated worst of all.

During the early years of Ezekiel's life, the government made laws which meant that Asiatics and Africans were not allowed to take skilled jobs. They could not earn much money and Africans were forced to live in Black-only areas of towns. Life became much worse in the early 1950s when the government, controlled by the Afrikaners, made apartheid laws. Apartheid is an Afrikaner word which means 'separate development' and the laws covered all areas of life. Africans could only be educated in 'traditional' ways, which meant that they could not get any advanced knowledge. Universities were for whites only. And new 'morality' laws stopped any marriages or relationships between people from different races. Africans could be sentenced[5] to death for having relationships with whites, for example. During this period South Africa left the British Commonwealth – the group of countries which used to be part of the British Empire.

Apartheid continued in South Africa until, after a long fight, a democracy was formed in 1994. There was African majority rule and the first president of the new South Africa was Nelson Mandela.

In this story of his early life, Ezekiel notices the effects of segregation[6] and unfair treatment, but he thinks that the things he sees around him are normal – it is just the way things are. He accepts that black people will always be ruled by white people and his family accepts this too. As he grows up and gets an education, he notices other things. Even among Africans, Ezekiel finds prejudice. In Natal, for example, he finds Zulu people who think that Sotho people like him are 'foreigners'. And he notices that the African people themselves have different views of the two groups of white people who oppress[7] them.

In the later part of the book, Ezekiel often writes about his studies. After his two years at Adams College where he trains to be a teacher, Ezekiel begins his university studies. He studies as an 'external student', which means that he studies at home and then takes examinations. First, he has to get a Matriculation Certificate, taking examinations in six subjects. This allows him to study for a general degree – a degree in several different subjects. Ezekiel obtains this general BA degree in English, Psychology and Native Administration. He goes on to take a BA Honours degree – a degree in one subject only. Ezekiel studies English for his Honours degree. Finally, he studies for an MA – a higher degree in English. For this degree, he has to write a thesis – a book – about a special subject. This book is not published, it is 'examined' by the university, and the thesis replaces the examinations of the lower degrees.

The book contains detailed descriptions of people Ezekiel knew, people he loved and people he hated. *Down Second Avenue* has been widely praised by critics for its moving description of life for black Africans in South Africa before democracy.

Cultural references and South African terms

Boer (page 12) someone whose family went from the Netherlands to live in South Africa. At the beginning of the 20th century, a war called The Anglo-Boer War (also known as the South African War) was fought in South Africa. The British defeated the Boers.

Native Commissioner (page 17) someone working at local government level responsible for the law, jobs and taxes

Location (page 19) a small town for people considered by the system of Apartheid to be black or coloured

my jong (page 25) a term that means 'my boy'

Kaffir (page 25) a very insulting word used to describe a black African person

Standard (page 26) the name for a school grade or year

stoep (page 27) a veranda or steps leading up to a house

Rand (page 28) a large area of land that runs from Gauteng in South Africa.

Don Quixote (page 37) a book written in the middle of the 17th century by the Spanish writer Cervantes. The hero is a man who believes in doing good things.

Tennyson (page 37) Lord Alfred Tennyson was a popular British poet. He was born in 1809 and died in 1892.

Byron (page 37) Lord George Byron was a popular British poet. He was born in 1788 and died in 1824.

Marabi (page 43) a new type of music that developed in Africa in the 1960s. Marabi was a mixture of jazz and blues music which was designed to encourage people to visit bars and dance. The authorities did not approve of this music.

sjambok (page 45) a strong, heavy whip – a long thin piece of leather with a handle on one end

Voortrekker (page 46) a member of a group of Afrikaner pioneers who left the British-ruled Cape in the early 19th century and moved to the interior of South Africa

Paul Kruger (page 47) State President of the South African Republic, famous for fighting against the British during the Anglo-Boer War of 1899–1902

Coolie (page 49) an insulting word used in the past for a worker from Asia with no special skills

Hertzog Bills (page 64) laws introduced by the government of the time, who believed in complete segregation on all levels: economic, political and educational. They caused a lot of misery for black South Africans.

Bantu (page 77) Bantu languages are a large group of related languages spoken in Central and Southern Africa.

1

Maupaneng and the Leshoana River

In the autumn of 1924, we – my brother, sister and I – were taken to the country to live with our grandmother – our father's mother. I have never known why our parents took us to live with her. Our parents didn't move with us. They stayed in the city of Pretoria, where they both worked. I was five years old.

We went to live in a little village called Maupaneng, about seventy-five miles from Pietersburg in north-eastern Transvaal. I felt very lonely during my first few weeks in the village. My grandmother was big and stern[8], and sat all day under a tree next to our hut. She never spoke kindly to me. She frightened me. The mountain near the village frightened me and the darkness frightened me too.

My parents bought two goats for us. I was happy because the goats seemed to know that we needed their company. They tickled[9] our hands when they ate the leaves which we gave them. One of the other families in the village kept their goats with ours. Sometimes a boy from that family and I looked after them and sometimes we went to school. We had to walk seven miles to school and seven miles back.

The school was one huge class in a big hall where we chanted multiplication tables[10] and the spellings of words. The teachers sometimes beat us with a stick so when I thought of school I thought of pain. I hated school and I preferred to help my grandmother and uncle in the fields. Sometimes they let me help them plough[11] the fields and chase away the birds from the crops, but only when they were very busy. I didn't believe I ought to go to school every day. None of the children did. But my family really wanted me to learn.

The goats seemed to know that we needed their company.

'You didn't go to school today, Eseki. I can see it in your eyes,' my grandmother said one day.

'I did, Granny,' I replied.

'Don't lie to me,' she said, in a bad mood.

My uncle, who lived with us, came in. 'You were not in school, Eseki, and you'd better not lie about it,' he said. He was so tall that he was like a tree standing over me.

It was true, I hadn't been to school. I had been in the mountains with my friends all day. My uncle beat me.

Sometimes I went with my friends to the river – the Leshoana. It was a broad river with white sand. It was a tame river except when it rained. Then it was fierce[12], this river. We boys went there in the moonlight and fought each other, or we hunted hares and rabbits. We came back at dawn and we laughed when someone was frightened by the noise of an owl.

————

The communal[13] fireplace was an important place. Men and boys of the village met there to talk, away from women and girls. We, the boys, had to bring wood for the fire. We brought it from the veld[14] when we brought back our goats. We learnt a lot at the fireplace, though at the time we didn't know that we were learning. We learnt about history, tradition and customs and the way to behave in a community. The old men told stories:

'When the Swazis fought with Bapedi …'

'When we lived under Boer rule …'

Old Segone was a great storyteller. He told us the story of Thema, a boy from a Christian family like ours. Thema had learnt that Jesus was our brother and that he died for us all. But trouble came for Thema when he went to the city to work for a white man. He came back and said that men were not brothers in the city. In the city, the black man must enter the white man's house through the back door. The black man cleans the streets but he mustn't walk on the pavement. The black man

12

builds houses for the white man but he cannot live in them. The black man cooks the white man's food but he only eats what is left over.

'Thema shocked us,' said Old Segone. 'He said, "Don't listen to anyone who tells you that black men and white men are brothers." And he said, "I don't know why Jesus Christ wasted his time teaching mankind." '

––––

When I look back to the first thirteen years of my life, I think that the time was wasted. Nobody shaped those years into a definite pattern. I search for a pattern now, and I remember a few things clearly – my grandmother, the mountain, the tropical darkness. I remember the long black tropical snakes, the fierce Leshoana River, the heavy rains and the heat. But probably I lived a life shared by all country boys. Country boys know only one purpose in life – to be.

I remember what we ate. Often our crops failed and we didn't have much to eat. Mother sent us a few tins of jam and we ate that with cornmeal porridge. Sometimes, she sent us sugar which we ate with porridge. Other times we cooked flying ants or hairy tree worms. The only time we tasted tea and bread was when our mother came to see us each Christmas. If the hunting was bad, we didn't eat meat. We had fifty goats but we didn't often kill one.

I also remember the vermin[15] – the bugs and lice were a nightmare. My grandmother had very clean habits. So did the rest of the people. But no one ever thought they could do anything about the bugs. They were big, flat, grey bugs which fell from the grass roof at night onto the mud floor of our hut. You scratched your naked body and you heard other people scratching too. But you couldn't catch the bugs on your body. In winter the bugs disappeared and in summer they came back. It never occurred to anyone that there might be a vermin killer.

We had one set of clothing for Sundays but on weekdays

we wore rags[16]. This was strange because Mother was a very good dressmaker. She sent clothes to our grandmother but our grandmother never gave them to us. She hid them away because she wanted us to be tough[17]. When my mother finally found the clothes, they were too small for us. I had to wear rags for weeks and weeks and they became a nest for lice. I sat out on the veld, picked off the eggs and crushed the lice between my fingernails. But I don't remember being ill very often. Sometimes I ate too many prickly pears and had a stomach ache – but that was all.

2

Into the Slums[18]

When I was about twelve, I noticed something that was happening in our part of north-eastern Transvaal. Young men were leaving the villages to work in the city of Pretoria. At Christmas, they came back to visit. They wore smart clothes and told us about the excitement of city life – the money (they earned three pounds a month), the electric lights, the trams and motor cars. Children didn't usually see these things until they were old enough to go to the city.

Because the younger men went to the city, there were mostly middle-aged women, old women and old men in our village. They did not have much land. The old men always complained that the white man had taken away most of it and they sat by the fire and looked helpless.

I never dreamt that I would go back to the city. Then, in the middle of the year, my mother came. She had come to take us back to Pretoria. I remember three things about the next few days. Firstly, my grandmother cried. Secondly, my mother took away our rags and gave us new clothes. Thirdly, I remember the bright lights on Pietersburg Station after a long journey on a dusty road. I was confused most of the time. At last we got to Pretoria Station and we went in a taxi to Marabastad, a black location. And that is how a country boy came to the city.

My other grandmother (my mother's mother), my Aunt Dora and three uncles lived on Second Avenue and we stayed with them for a few days. Then, my brother and sister and I went to live on Fifth Avenue in one room with my mother and father. I was now thirteen years old. My brother was three years younger than me and my sister was five years younger.

I noticed quickly that things were not right between my

mother and father. They argued a lot about money. My mother worked hard. She made dresses for a tailor[19] during the day and in the evening she made beer which she sold. My father did not bring any money home. He drank the beer my mother made with his friends. My mother got very angry but she couldn't do anything about it.

My father was a violent man with a thin and bony face that I didn't like. He limped[20] all the time because he had hurt his leg in an accident when he was younger. He did not play with us often and we stayed close to my mother most of the time. There were five people in our room but there was a sixth companion – fear.

'I don't want that man here again. Do you hear me, Eva?' my father said one evening. He was talking about the man who lived in the next room.

'He's *your* friend and you know he comes here to drink,' my mother answered. She told us to go outside, as she often did when my father got angry.

'Don't talk to me like that! Didn't your mother teach you not to answer back to your husband?' we heard him say.

'You started the argument, Moses.'

We looked through the window. My father hit my mother. A crashing slap made her fall on her knees.

'I'll kill you, I tell you!' he shouted.

We didn't sleep well that night.

'Why does Father do this to you always, Mother?' I asked one day.

'I don't know, Son,' she replied. She didn't really want to talk about it. She never complained to us.

I hated my father and so did my brother and sister. Once he called us to him – it was a drunken call. 'Eseki, Girlie, Solomon!' He put his arms round us. 'I – I – I – brought you sweets, see? From – from the town.' My mother laughed. Then she laughed again when he said, 'Remember you're my oldest child, Eseki. You are my heir[21] and you will inherit everything I have. Don't let anyone cheat you out of it.'

I slowly learnt from my mother why she had brought us to the city from Maupaneng. My father had refused to give her any money for us. She had reported him to the Native Commissioner. The Commissioner had advised her to get us from the country.

'If the children live with you and their father, he will remember to pay for them,' he had said.

My mother had to report regularly to the Commissioner. She told me not to worry. 'You're young and these things are too heavy for your small shoulders,' she said.

I remember one Sunday morning. Sunday was the day when we stayed in bed, wrapped in our blankets. The gas from the primus stove[22] made a soft noise. There was a good smell of meat, potatoes and curry from a pot on the stove. I was thinking of Maupaneng. I was thinking of the big dark mountains, the fields, my friends and the old men telling stories. I could see through the window that it was cloudy. I hated clouds then and I still hate clouds today. They made me feel sad and grey, in Maupaneng and in Pretoria.

I heard running footsteps. I suddenly stopped day-dreaming and my brother woke up. My mother ran into the room and tripped over a piece of wood. She fell on her knees near the door. My father ran into the house behind her and we knew he was chasing her. She stayed on her knees and I knew she had hurt herself.

'I'll show you who I am!' my father shouted.

'What's the matter with you, Moses? What are you doing?' she said.

'Get up!' he shouted.

'I can't – I can't – my knee hurts!' my mother cried.

'This is the day when you are going to do what I tell you!' He limped over to the pot on the stove and poured the contents of the pot over her. My mother screamed in a voice I have never forgotten. Hot potatoes and meat and curry covered her blouse. Then my father caught hold of her blouse with one hand and crashed the pot onto her head with the other. It made a heavy sound, like a large bell. She freed herself from him and ran out of the door, crying.

At last I realized what was happening and ran for help. An ambulance took my mother to hospital and the police arrested my father. We packed our bags and went to live with my grandmother on Second Avenue.

A few weeks later my mother came out of hospital. I went with her to court[23] for the trial of my father and my mother told the magistrate the story of that Sunday morning and many other things about my father. The magistrate sentenced him to fourteen days in prison or a fine. I don't remember how much the fine was but I know he paid the money. The summer of 1932 was the last time I ever saw my father. The strong smell of burning gas from a primus stove often reminds me of that Sunday morning.

3

Marabastad Location

The water from our communal tap ran very slowly into containers. Everyone had to wait in a queue at the water tap. The water trickled[24] into tin cans, buckets and dishes, and the people waited. Sometimes you heard someone make a noise of impatience. Sometimes people argued. Sometimes they laughed and gossiped[25]. Some people sat on their tins and some people fed their babies. It was like this in Second Avenue. And you knew that it was like this at every communal water tap in Marabastad.

The houses were a little like our tin cans too, because they were made of corrugated iron[26]. The streets were straight and the houses stood very close together. Each house had a fence made with posts and wire that didn't stand up straight. The fences swayed[27] like drunken men. Most houses had a veranda[28] with a mud floor. The verandas had roofs which were unevenly supported with four wooden poles. The backyards of the houses were usually dirty though people swept them continually with grass brooms. Most of the people with houses rented rooms to a family or to single people. So there might be several families' coal braziers[29] burning in the same yard. In the mornings and afternoons, Marabastad was always covered by a blanket of smoke from these braziers.

There was a white superintendent of the location who we called Ra-Stand. We only saw him when we went to pay our fourteen shillings rent or when he drove up the main road, Barber Street. Otherwise the location seemed to belong to the police, the dirty water, the flies, the dead cats and dogs and children's faeces[30]. We didn't see many white people. We saw the white superintendent and the police, and white ministers

You knew that it was like this at every communal water tap in Marabastad.

from the Methodist or Anglican churches or sometimes a school superintendent. A white person never came to the location unless he was in charge of something. I never thought that this was strange. I don't think any other Marabastad resident thought this was strange either.

For a while, Marabastad was like a foreign country to my brother and sister and me. Why did people build houses in a straight line? Why did they build fences between houses? Why did adults go to the toilet in a bucket in a small building? We asked ourselves these things. It was very different from Maupaneng. In the village, houses didn't stand in straight lines. People visited one another. They told stories around the communal fire. But gradually we realized that there was a community in Marabastad. The people didn't *seem* to be interested in one another, but they were. We slowly got used to life on Second Avenue.

My mother, Aunt Dora and three uncles were born in eastern Transvaal. Aunt Dora, her three children and the three uncles lived with us and our grandmother. Mother, who was the eldest, worked in one of the white suburbs of Pretoria as a servant. She lived there and came to see us on two Sundays in a month. We had two rooms. One room was a bedroom. One room, which had a table and four chairs, was both a bedroom and a sitting-room. There were two other rooms in the house which we rented to tenants.

There was a ten-foot-wide yard all round the house. Flowers wouldn't grow in the yard, but we did have a grape-vine creeper[31] which gave shade to the person who was doing the washing. There was a path from the gate to the front and to the back of the house. This was made with mud and animal dung[32], and small pebbles were pressed into it in a pattern. We planted maize in the front yard and about seven corn cobs grew each year. We children were given half a cob each to eat which we cooked on the back veranda.

In the morning, we had coffee. Afterwards, we often had mealie-meal[33] porridge made from food left over from last night's supper. After school, I had to clean our house because Grandmother and Aunt Dora did white people's washing all day to earn money. I had to make a fire and buy a small piece of meat – usually about one pound in weight – from an Indian butcher's shop in the Asiatic reserve. There were so many of us in the family that I had to cook porridge twice in the same big pot. On weekdays, our supper was simple – porridge and meat – but when there was no money we fried tomatoes. On Sundays, we ate some vegetables with our meat. We only had butter when we had visitors. We bought three-pence worth[34]. Then our grandmother gave each child one slice of bread with a thin layer of butter on it. The adults ate their meals from saucers while we children shared a plate. We never sat at the table to eat.

On Monday mornings, at about four o'clock, I went to the white suburbs to collect washing for Grandmother and Aunt Dora. On Thursday and Friday afternoons, I had to take the washing back. Sometimes I could borrow a bike, but other times I had to walk. It was about seven miles and I carried the bundles of washing on my head. I had a pair of tennis shoes but I was not allowed to wear these on weekdays – they were for Sundays. In the winter, my bare feet hurt.

One winter morning, I was cycling home from Waterkloof suburb with a large bundle of washing on the handlebars. I was wearing a thin jacket and I was very, very cold. From the opposite direction a group of white boys came cycling towards me. I couldn't turn the handlebars very well because of the washing. I crashed into the first boy who fell onto the next boy and he then fell onto the boy next to him. My bicycle hit the pavement and I fell off.

'Bastard[35],' shouted the boy who had fallen off first.

His friends all came and kicked and cursed[36] me. Then they

22

rode away. They left me on the ground in pain and in the cold. The bicycle had a bent front wheel.

My friends laughed when I told them. 'You country sheep. That's your first lesson. You've got to go about town with your eyes open,' one of them said.

4

Saturday Night

It was a Saturday night. The street lights were on and there was a misty light over Marabastad. Everyone was watchful, especially the women. I was watching for the light from torches. I think now that the torchlight was very threatening. It was always like this for us: Saturday night and police torches, Saturday night and police whistles, Saturday night and screams, Saturday night and cursing from the white man. And I was only thirteen.

We made beer at our house. We put the beer into large oil cans. The white man did not allow the black man to have beer so the oil cans had to be hidden. I watched for the policemen's torch. If a policeman came, the beer had to be put in a hole in the ground quickly.

It was always like this. The white man did not let the black woman make beer even though she used the money to pay for her children to go to school.

'Go and watch outside,' my aunt told me.

'Dig the hole deep,' said my mother. 'Stamp hard on the earth.'

It was always like this. You are on the white man's land; you must do his washing; you must buy bread from him with the money he pays you; you must live in houses built by him; he must control your area.

One night, I was waiting outside the house for the last oil can of beer from my mother when I heard heavy footsteps. She handed me the oil can through the window before the footsteps came round the corner into the backyard. I threw the can over the fence into a big container of dirty water. A white policeman and an African policeman came round the corner and suddenly there was a blinding white light in my face. I was terrified and my body shook.

'What are you doing here "my jong"?' the big white policeman asked in Afrikaans. He switched off his terrible light.

'Nothing,' I said.

'How can you stand here alone and do nothing, Kaffir?'

I said nothing. I thought about my mother in the house, clearing away the evidence of beer-making.

'What was that I heard when I came in?' asked the white policeman.

'I was throwing a stone at a dog.' I answered. I had to keep them in the yard until my mother had tidied up inside.

'Hold the bastard's arms behind his back, Jonas,' said the white policeman. Then his big white hand crashed into my cheek. I fell against a fence pole and the black man pulled me away so hard that my side hurt.

'Are you going to tell me the truth, Kaffir?' the white policeman asked.

I didn't answer. I didn't care now. 'Let anything happen,' I thought.

The back of the white policeman's hand hit me across my mouth. While I held my mouth, he got hold of my neck and pressed my face against his other hand. I couldn't breathe.

'That was for your lies, Kaffir,' he said. And he pushed me away from him. I fell down on the ground.

Then the sound of their footsteps became quieter. I felt sick. Everything became black in front of me. But the people in Marabastad continued to make beer. The police continued to raid[37] the location and destroy the beer.

5

School and Friends

Everybody knew that schools in the country were not very good. So they did not expect me to be good at the school in the location. The class teacher, the principal and my aunt all said I was backward, so I had to believe it. They put me in Standard Three, not Standard Four – the Standard which was right for my age. I didn't think that they could be wrong. I was in a class of eighty children. In the first test I was 77th in the class and no one at home was surprised.

At last, I went up to Standard Four. The class teacher had a nickname – 'Kuzwi'. He was a small man who beat us very often with a cane[38]. He rang the bell to start the class when we were a long way from the school. He did this to make us late for class. Then he beat us. If you were 50th in one test and 51st in the next one, he caned you. If you cycled to school, he caned you because you didn't walk there. We were very happy when we went up to Standard Five and had a different teacher.

Life in the city still surprised me. One day, I was with my friend, Moloi, who lived next door. He was a happy person who liked to sing. We were going to the movies and I stopped to look up at a tall building which wasn't finished yet.

'Come on, you sheep!' Moloi said. 'We're going to be late. Haven't you ever seen a building?'

The building was as high as the mountains back in Maupaneng and I was a bit frightened.

'Don't you think it will fall over soon, Moloi?' I asked.

'Don't be silly. These white people are clever, you know. They do all the thinking about these things,' Moloi said.

'What do you mean? The blacks do all the work in the north where I come from,' I replied.

'This is not the north, chum[39],' he said. 'I tell you – the whites do all the thinking here.'

'Like the man who gave me a slap at the market this morning?' I asked.

'Yes, chum,' said Moloi. And he laughed and laughed.

The market manager had slapped me on the back of my head that morning. Moloi and I had been picking up carrots and over-ripe tomatoes when he caught us. We were going to eat them while we pushed a cart of vegetables to the suburbs for a white customer.

I had been hungry and depressed all day. Was life always going to be like this?

But I forgot my hunger and depression when we got to the movies. We saw a lot of movies for fourpence. They were silent films and we saw lots of funny actors like Harold Lloyd, Charlie Chaplin and Buster Keaton. We stood on our chairs and cheered, and a piano played noisy tunes.

I read the dialogue and titles from the screen for the other boys. When I did this, I felt big and important and useful. Often I didn't have money for the movies. Then one of the boys paid for me so that I could read for them. I had 'gone into business'!

'How do you read so fast?' asked Moloi.

'Because I can,' I said mysteriously.

'It's no use asking you anything,' he answered. He was angry with me.

The truth was that I read everything. I picked up any piece of paper to read. I felt inferior to my classmates at school because I was not very good at English and all our lessons were in English. But I read and read. I felt proud because soon I would not be backward any more.

———

A group of boys from Second Avenue used to meet on the stoep of a shop on Barber Street after school. We called ourselves the Foxes. There was me and Moloi, little Links and China, Ratau and Danie, the noisiest boy on Second Avenue, and a few other boys. There was also Isaac who came from Bantule, another location two miles away. He went to school with us and liked to play with the Foxes. We talked about school and the cane.

There were three Chinese shops and five Indian shops along Barber Street. The Chinese shops were grocery shops built from corrugated iron. The Indian shops were bigger buildings, built from brick and Abdool's was one of these. There was fruit in one window and in the other window, there were dusty plates and tiny toys. There was always a lovely spicy smell. At night, when the alarm for the curfew[40] went at ten minutes to ten, Abdool's servants covered the windows with wooden shutters and iron bars. There was a curfew on Africans from 11.00 p.m. to 4.30 a.m.

One day we were standing on the stoep when a girl walked past. We had never seen her before. She walked quickly, swinging[41] her arms, as if she might be able to fly.

'Who's she?' Moloi asked.

'She's the new girl who moved into our street with her father yesterday. Don't you know that?' replied China, as if everyone should know.

'She's got a cheek [P], she has,' said Moloi, quite angrily.

'Why?' I asked.

'She came to this place yesterday. She hasn't asked where the shops are or where the school is or where the police station is,' said Moloi.

'Perhaps she comes from the Rand,' suggested Ratau.

'My father says nobody asks anybody anything on the Rand,' Links said.

'The Rand's a strange place,' said China.

'I've got an idea, Foxes,' said Moloi. 'If she asks you anything, look away. Is that agreed?'

'Yes,' everyone answered.

When she passed us again there was silence. She walked down Barber Street, round the corner and into Second Avenue and she didn't notice us.

'What a cheeky face!' I thought.

We soon got to know about the new girl, Rebone, and her father, Dinku Dikae. Ma-Lebona, who lived across the street from us, came to talk about them to my grandmother. She always came to talk to my grandmother when she wanted to gossip.

'Everybody says he's a very rich man,' said Ma-Lebona. 'But he doesn't look like a rich man, Hibila. I said to him that we are happy to see them and we hope they will be happy in our quiet street. And do you know what, Hibila?'

'U-huh?' said my grandmother.

'The little girl looked at me straight in the face – straight in the face!' Ma-Lebone continued. 'She looked as if she was going to say – "I'll scratch your eyes out ᴾ if you come near my father."'

'You wouldn't *want* to be with him, would you?' Aunt Dora asked.

'Dora! How can you say such a thing?' she replied. She was shocked.

Rebone's father was about forty years old when they came to Second Avenue and Rebone was the same age as the Foxes, thirteen. Dinku Dikae was strong with broad shoulders and big arms but Rebone was small and cat-like. She had big dark eyes and a small waist – like a wasp's[42] waist, I thought. Ma-Lebona thought she was like a wasp too.

'God knows, Hibila,' she said to my grandmother. 'One day she will go "ving, ving, ving," like a wasp over our heads. Beware of that girl! My blood tells me something.'

Soon Dinku Dikae became a hawker – he started a business selling fruit and vegetables from a cart – and Rebone joined us in Standard Five at school. She wasn't shy and she soon made a lot of friends.

One day at school, when we were all tired because of the midsummer heat, I wrote a note which said: *I love you, Eseki.* I asked someone behind me to hand it to Rebone. I was copying history notes from the board when suddenly I felt a hard slap behind my ear. When I turned round I saw Rebone sitting down again in her seat. When our eyes met, she made an angry hissing noise, like a snake. It's a noise that only African girls can make.

But in a few weeks' time, it had become a habit for me to carry Rebone's books when we walked home together. She told me a lot about the Rand – the Golden City – the big city of Johannesburg.

6

Ma-Lebona and Other People

Our neighbour, Ma-Lebona, was about fifty. She was thin and she looked as if she was made of tight pieces of string. She went to the houses in Second Avenue giving advice to men and women even if they didn't want it. She always looked people in their eyes. She boasted[43] that she looked everybody directly in their eyes – black or white. Women who were the same age as her thought this was very brave behaviour for an African woman.

'A good wife must obey her mother-in-law. She must be able to wash, cook, clean the house and look after the children well,' she often said. 'But the young girls we have now for daughters-in-law are stupid and stubborn[44].'

Ma-Lebona had been married twice, I heard Aunt Dora tell a friend. Her first husband stayed with her for three years, then he left her. Her second husband stayed for two years before leaving her. They had a daughter who stayed with Ma-Lebona. The husband was sorry about that, said Aunt Dora. He didn't want anything on earth to remind him of Ma-Lebona. Then there was a third man in Ma-Lebona's life who lived with her but did not marry her. They had a son, Joel, and the man stayed with them for ten years before he left Marabastad.

After the men had left, Ma-Lebona went into the business of controlling daughters-in-law.

Ma-Lebona's two children, Nkati and Joel, didn't go higher at school than Standard Eight, but she still boasted about them.

'I have two children at Kilnerton High School,' she used to say to her neighbours. 'You have to work, work, work to get them through school. I don't know what I will do when they

31

go to Fort Hare!' Fort Hare was the only non-white university college in South Africa in those days.

The children were very different from each other. Their mother was strict with them both, but Nkati was rebellious and would not obey her mother. Joel always obeyed her. We often went to stay at Ma-Lebona's house when the adult members of our family were away for a few days. I was embarrassed by the way Joel said, 'Yes, Ma', 'I will, Ma,' 'All right, Ma', to everything she said.

When Nkati met a young man, she left home. She married him and went to live on Fourteenth Avenue.

'I asked them many times to live with me,' Ma-Lebona said to my grandmother one day. 'But the boy said to Nkati that he would not be controlled by his mother-in-law.'

'And what did she say?' asked my grandmother.

'She said that she belongs to *him* now,' she replied. 'It's not like it was when I was a girl. In those days, the parents told the girl that the first baby must be born at home. I told her that the anger of her ancestors[45] will fall on her one day.'

I don't know if the ancestors' anger ever fell on Nkati. But I do know that about eight out of ten educated Africans, most of whom are Christians, still believe in the spirits of their ancestors.

Joel, however, married a girl his mother had chosen – the daughter of an old friend.

'No, child, that stove is not clean,' Ma-Lebona said to her. 'No, child, you must not sit like that when you are pregnant,' she said. 'Joel likes his egg boiled not fried,' she said. 'Joel does not drink tea,' she said. This was how she talked to her daughter-in-law. Anna, Joel's wife, obeyed without question. She behaved as all new wives are told to do by their aunts and uncles on their wedding day.

'Anna's ready to explode,' said Aunt Dora one day, like someone who has been expecting it for a long time. 'I went to borrow some sugar and she was arguing with Ma-Lebona. "You mustn't argue with Mother, Anna," Joel kept saying to her.'

Ma-Lebona told all the neighbours about her daughter-in-law's bad behaviour, then one day Aunt Dora came in and said, 'She's done it!'

'Who? What?' we asked.

'Anna. She has slapped her mother-in-law on the cheek.'

Everyone on Second Avenue was shocked. Some people said, 'It's good for Ma-Lebona. She's met her match p!'

Then finally Anna left.

'She told me herself,' said Aunt Dora. 'Joel will never keep a wife because a wife has to be his mother's wife as well.'

We all looked forward to Joel's next wedding to Kuku, who was a pretty woman. The bells rang and the church filled up with people. The minister was waiting and Joel, the bridegroom, arrived. But the bride, pretty Kuku, never came. 'A car with Johannesburg number plates picked her up at her house,' people said.

'God knows best,' Aunt Dora said, 'but that sweet girl was never meant for Joel.'

———

I remember very well some of the white people in the suburbs whose washing I collected. There was Mr Goldsmith, who was a middle-aged man with a very red face. He worked at the museum where Aunt Dora's husband also worked. He could easily have brought the washing to the museum in his car. Then I could have collected it from the centre of the city instead of going all the way to the suburbs. But he never thought of it. He was always angry. Often he didn't answer the door, but he cursed if I knocked on the window. And then, as I waited under the window, he opened it and threw the bundle at me. He wouldn't look at me. At the end of the month, he threw the envelope containing money at me. He did not care whether I caught it or not.

He opened it and threw the bundle at me.

Miss Forster was an alcoholic who looked very old. She always complained to me about things that did not concern me. She complained about the weather and about the noise her neighbours made when they played Afrikaner music at the weekend. She also complained about her brother in Johannesburg who had not sent her money. We called her Ma-Bottles because every week she sent me to a bottle store on my way home. I got a shilling for doing this so I didn't mind.

At Mrs Singer's house, they let me wait in the kitchen while they collected up the bundle of washing. I often sat there with saliva in my mouth because of the warm smell of coffee and eggs and ham. We never had food like this at home. I always remember the dog and the attention they gave it. 'The girl', as they called their black maid who was probably twenty-five years old, gave the dog a bowl of fresh tea after its breakfast. Mrs Singer was always shouting at 'the girl' for not treating the dog well. One day there was another 'girl' working for the Singers because the first 'girl' had been sacked for beating their dog. Since that time, I have never wanted to keep pets.

Big Eyes, the Headmaster

The schools in Marabastad were run by the different religious groups and I went to the Methodist School. The Methodist School had a large hall, built of iron and wood, where Standards One, Two and Three of primary school were taught. Then there was a little brick hall where Standards Four and Five were taught. And for Standard Six there was a little wood and iron building which looked as if it was going to fall down. In each class, pupils sat three to a small desk. There were old blackboards on which the teachers wrote.

When I was in Standard Five, Rebone and I started competing for first place in the class. Sometimes she was in first place and I was in second place. Sometimes I was in first place and she was in second place. It was as if we had an agreement to do this. For the first time in my primary school career I felt self-confident.

Then, when I was fifteen, I passed Standard Five and went into Standard Six. I had never liked arithmetic[46] and I still hated it but my love of reading grew stronger. The white family my mother worked for gave me old newspapers and magazines. They just gave them to my mother for me; they weren't interested in me as a person. I was disappointed because I thought they should be interested in someone who wanted to be like them – someone who wanted to be educated and read a lot. I was very proud that I was able to read English.

My mother was very, very proud of me and my progress but she could only afford to buy me the two reading books for school – a book in English and a book in Sotho. I looked all the time for books which had been thrown away – old, tattered[47], rat-eaten, sun-damaged books. Once I found a tattered copy of

Don Quixote which I read three times before the pages fell out. I also enjoyed the poetry we read at school. We learnt poems by English poets like Tennyson and Byron for oral examinations in front of the school inspectors and we liked the poems so much that we also read them out at concerts.

In Standard Six, I felt as if a great light had come on inside me. It was like the dawn of a new day [P]. Even though life was very hard at home, I felt that my school career had begun to make sense. I was well ahead of my classmates in all subjects except arithmetic. Rebone dropped to three places behind me. 'We told you she couldn't last,' said the bigger boys, but I knew what was wrong. Rebone was teaching her father to read and write and do simple arithmetic because she had found out that his business was doing badly. Vegetable and fruit prices in the market were rising and he couldn't afford them. Rebone also told me that her father was scared of the police.

We called our headmaster Big Eyes because his eyes were always huge and staring. On Monday mornings, Big Eyes always enjoyed coming to the large school hall. On the day after the weekend he caned students in front of the whole school. He caned students who he had caught at a Saturday dance or a Sunday afternoon party. He caught people because he often dressed up like a woman and went to a party or a dance. He knew all his students even though there were three hundred of us in Standards One to Six.

A lot of people thought Big Eyes was a good headmaster.

'Give me a man who will clean the human rubbish off the streets,' said one.

'That's right! Boys and girls are changing,' said others. 'They are cheeky, they have no respect for their parents and they go to the Columbia Dance Hall. They have children when they are children themselves. He's the headmaster who will help us.'

37

Grandmother was one of the people who praised Big Eyes but she stopped praising him when he caned me. It was in 1934, just after I had started Standard Six, and he caned me because I didn't go to a school choir practice. The choir was practising for the visit of the son of the King of England, Prince George, to South Africa. I had not gone to the practice because I had to collect washing from the suburbs. I explained this but I was still caned. Grandmother was not going to do anything about my caning but Aunt Dora came to school with me.

'Why did you beat Es'ki yesterday, Headmaster, when he told you he went to collect the washing?' she asked Big Eyes.

'What do you expect me to do if every student makes an excuse for not coming to choir practice?' he replied.

'I am talking about Es'ki, not the other children,' she said. 'I don't care what you do to the other children.'

'This is a difficult time and we must learn the songs before the Prince comes,' said Big Eyes.

'So the washing cannot be collected because the Prince is coming? Is the Prince going to buy food for my family?' replied Aunt Dora.

'Can't the boy collect it another day?' asked Big Eyes.

I wanted very much to be in the choir and I hoped that my aunt would say that I could collect the washing another day.

'No, he can't,' she said. 'You had no right to punish[48] the boy before you found out he was telling the truth.'

Big Eyes looked surprised and took a step backwards. 'I know how to run my school, Madam,' he said.

'And I know how to run my family,' my aunt replied. 'If this happens another time, I will speak to the superintendent. Now go to your class, Es'ki.'

The superintendent of every church school was a white minister who led the white religious services of the church that ran the school.

38

I had to collect the washing on the normal day so I couldn't sing in the choir. But I was in the scout division[49] that marched past the Prince which was exciting and I enjoyed it. I also enjoyed the cold drinks and cakes which were given to us on the 'Non-Europeans Only' celebration day. There had already been a 'Europeans Only' day.

8

The Columbia Dance Hall

In the early nineteen thirties, there was a depression which did not seem on the surface to make the black man's poverty[50] any worse. There was still only one proper road for the white superintendent of the location to drive his shiny car along. There were still no electric lights in the houses. But the poverty did get worse. White people didn't want to pay us as much as they once did. They brought down the price from nine pence to six pence for carrying vegetables five miles to a suburb.

There was much less to eat at home and boys and girls raided the Indian hawkers' backyards for old bread and fruit and vegetables. The Foxes – Links and Danie, Ratau and China, Moloi and Isaac and I – went to raid various yards. At the end of the raids, we went to wash the oranges, carrots, tomatoes and other items; all of it was black and rotten and we washed it as well as we could. Twice a week, we took sacks and made the long walk to the city's ash dump in the last suburb west of the town. We searched for lumps of coke to use in the braziers at home and came back white because we were covered with ash.

During this time, I began to realize that the Indian people had more money than us. We never really got to know them. There were barriers between us all.

Another change in the depression years was that boys of our age began to get rough and 'knife-happy'. Many of them left school and joined the people who couldn't or wouldn't get jobs. They called themselves 'bright boys' and formed gangs who fought each other: XY Ranch, Jumbo Ranch, Frisco Ranch, Texas Ranch, Express Ranch, Uppercut Ranch. They stopped men in the street and pointed the knives at them. Then they undressed them completely and left them naked. They sold the clothes. The boys robbed anyone they could find.

'The world is coming to an end,' said my grandmother with a sigh, 'as sure as Titus sleeps in his grave.' Titus was my grandfather, her husband. 'When I was young there wasn't so much hate. Boys and girls didn't insult[51] their elders and we helped each other when times were bad. The world is nearing an end.' She frightened me when she talked in this way.

Boeta Lem (Brother Blade) was one of the worst of the young men. He collected a big group of men around him and they talked about what the gangs did 'on the Rand'.

'If I see you listening to what Boeta Lem says, I'll cut your neck into pieces with an axe,' my grandmother said to us.

One day, a rich old man called Rametse came to our house, waving his arms in the air. 'He's done it again,' he shouted. 'He's done it to me this time. He's the son of a rat, the son of a pig.'

'Who's that?' my grandmother asked.

'That piece of dirt called Boeta Lem. He's stolen all my money from under my mattress. My woman saw him. She saw him run out of the house. I've worked for years for that money.' No one really knew how rich old Rametse was but people spoke of his richness as a fact.

'Go to the police station,' suggested Aunt Dora.

'Where do you think I am going?' he shouted.

The police took Boeta Lem to the police station but they could not or would not keep him there.

'God's no fool,' said my grandmother. 'That young man will fall over one day. You'll see.'

All the old people believed her. 'God will deal with him,' they said.

It seemed that God did catch up with Boeta Lem. One Saturday night he threatened a teenage girl with a knife and led her away from a cinema to a dark field. Then he raped[52] her. The girl ran home and the police were called. They found Boeta Lem at the Columbia Dance Hall. He still had the girl's underwear in his pocket. He was taken to the police station but his father got him a lawyer[53] and then he was bailed[54].

The next week, on a Sunday, the people of Second Avenue went to Boeta Lem's home, where he lived with his father and stepmother. They were angry that Boeta Lem had been given bail. Aunt Dora and I went with them. The crowd shouted:

'Let him come out!'

'Let us see him!'

'We don't want animals here! We want to take him back to the police station.'

At last Boeta Lem's father came out of his poor corrugated iron house with his son's hand in his. I remember how dignified Boeta Lem's father looked even though he was so unhappy. 'God's people,' he said, 'what do you want of me?'

'We want your son. He must go back to the police station,' a woman said. 'You shouldn't keep a criminal in your house and get a lawyer for him.'

'If he'd raped a white girl, he'd have been kept in the police station,' said another. 'Then he would be hanged[55].'

For a few minutes, Boeta Lem's father did not know what to say. Then he said, 'God's people, hear me. Some of you have children. You're lucky that some of them are not like this boy here. It hurts me when my boy makes life miserable for other people. I get a hundred stabs in my heart for every stab he gives his victim with his knife. You say that I like his crime because I paid for a lawyer for him.'

He paused and I could see he was crying. His son stood beside him wearing a dirty tattered vest. He looked frightened.

'If you think that, you are cruel,' Boeta Lem's father continued. 'Why did I hire a lawyer for my son? I don't know. I can't tell you.'

'What about my money?' said old Rametse.

'That is a matter for the police,' replied the father. 'I have brought my son outside with me so that he can see what people think of his evil behaviour.'

The crowd of people started to move away.

'We leave you to tie up your own dog then,' one said.

Later, Boeta Lem appeared in court and he was sentenced to ten years' hard labour[56] in prison.

––––

The Columbia Dance Hall was in the centre of a row of Indian houses in the Asiatic Bazaar between Marabastad and the Coloured reserve. It was an old building with walls that were repainted very often to make it look attractive. We often did jobs for the manager of the Columbia in order to earn a few shillings and we examined every part of the building. The Columbia was a place that few parents liked. They told us it was an evil place where immoral[57] behaviour went on when there was a concert or a dance. Boys whose families did not watch them as closely as mine watched me told me about it. I promised myself that I would find out what my grandmother and Aunt Dora didn't want me to see.

Finally, the night came to find out about the Columbia. Talking pictures had just arrived in Pretoria and a new cinema, the Star Picture Palace, opened in the Asiatic Bazaar. It was showing a movie called *The Singing Fool* and I was allowed to go with Aunt Dora and two of my uncles. There was something on every night at the Columbia so this was my best chance of finding out what went on. But I loved the movies and I didn't want to miss this one. I was given my ticket and I rushed to the Columbia. I just had time to go inside while they showed the short films before *The Singing Fool*. I paid my shilling and I was let into the Columbia.

There was the noisy sound of 'Marabi' jazz. I stood against the wall. I saw all the dust that rose from the floor and the dim lights. I smelt tobacco smoke and sweat. Couples were dancing, holding each other very tightly. Their faces were wet with sweat and sometimes they wiped it off with the back of their hands. They swayed to the sound of the music. This was the Columbia, the terrible place. I ran out of the dance hall and into the cinema feeling very guilty. What would happen to me if my family found out I'd been there?

I enjoyed the film and a few weeks later we saw Charlie Chaplin's *City Lights*. Soon posters advertising films with 'talking, singing, dancing' were everywhere. At first I was worried by the talking pictures – perhaps I would go out of business! My friends wouldn't need me to read the titles on the screen anymore. They would be able to listen to the dialogue. But soon I just enjoyed the films we went to see together.

This was Marabastad during the depression years. Lots of jazz bands appeared and people found ways to enjoy themselves in spite of their poverty. Preachers in churches spoke out against the immorality. They preached sermons[58] against places like the Columbia and said there would be eternal punishment. My grandmother took us to the Methodist church because our mother was a Methodist. Then she and Aunt Dora and the rest of the family went to the Lutheran Church because my grandfather had been a Lutheran. But fewer people were going to church in those days and the preachers blamed people's immorality for this. Women, old men and children of our age went to church. The young men and women stayed away. The depression was God's punishment for all the immorality, the preachers said.

At this time, I made a decision to go to different churches on Sundays. I just loved change and I liked listening to sermons from different preachers. I loved the music of the Lutherans. I loved the fine clothes in the Anglican church. I liked listening to the African Methodist Episcopal preacher who mixed English and Sotho in his sermons. My grandmother thought he was mad but I just thought he was funny.

I told my grandmother about my uncertainty. She said I would end up going to no church at all. 'You'll be a heathen[59] like your father,' she said. But she didn't sound very cross.

Hundreds of young men and women were coming to Pretoria from northern Transvaal to find work. On Sundays, the young men came from the suburbs to Bantule, near Marabastad. Bantule was their playground. White policemen on horses led them through Marabastad. We called them *malaita* – Sotho for rough people. At the playground, they formed a circle, then pairs of them fought each other with their bare fists. It was bloody and brutal. When the fighting finished, the crowd broke up and returned to the suburbs. The police chased them and beat them with sjamboks. The police were supposed to stop the malaita from coming through the locations but they always came. None of us felt sorry for them as the police beat them. We chased them and threw sticks and stones and followed them until they left Marabastad. But every Sunday they left their masters' houses in the suburbs to behave badly in our area!

9

The Fight with Abdool

The children of some of the English-speaking families my mother worked for often came and stared at me. I never got used to being stared at like that. My mother learnt English but she refused to learn Afrikaans and always worked for English-speaking people. Aunt Dora washed clothes for Afrikaners. Even though I could speak Afrikaans fairly well, most families that Aunt Dora worked for wouldn't even let me in their kitchen. Their children looked out of the windows at me but usually they didn't take any notice of me. It felt better than being stared at. Sometimes they said, 'Ma, die wasgoed Kaffir is hier – Mummy, the washing Kaffir has come.'

I learnt that it was best to keep out of the white man's way. If a group of them walked next to each other on a pavement, we had to step onto the road. We could go to places like the museum or the zoo on certain days. There were no whites on those days so it was easier for us and we were happy enough. But we blacks couldn't even go near the fence of a park. Sometimes, we pressed our faces against a fence and watched the white children playing on swings. When the white park keeper shouted at us, I hated him. I hated the children too, because I was jealous of them.

In South Africa, 16th December was Dingaan's Day. This was a public holiday on the same day that the Boer leader Piet Retief and his men had been killed by Dingaan, the terrible Zulu king. On that day, Afrikaner men rode through the centre of Pretoria on horses. Many of the men had fought in the Anglo-Boer War and they wore Voortrekker clothing, large hats and big bandoliers[60]. Large crowds stood on the pavements on either side of the road and admired them.

On Dingaan's Day in 1934, I came from the suburbs and saw Rebone near the crowds. She told me she had been to the station with her aunt who was going to Johannesburg by train.

'Let's go and look at the horses,' she said.

'I'm scared,' I replied.

'Come on, Es'ki.' She pulled me by the arm and soon we were inside the crowd. We hadn't been standing there long when a huge Afrikaner said, 'Get away, Kaffir! This is not a monkey show.'

'We're only looking,' said Rebone.

Suddenly, the Afrikaner got hold of me by the back of my neck. Another hand slapped me on the cheek a few times. Something hit me on my nose. Someone kicked me in the back and I fell out of the crowd and onto the street. Rebone soon joined me. We didn't speak for a while.

'The stinking Boers!' she cried angrily.

'It's your fault,' I replied. 'We had no right to go into that crowd, we shouldn't have gone in.'

There were tears in my eyes and I felt so bitter that I couldn't speak anymore. But deep inside me I felt very proud of Rebone.

When we talked about how bad things were with the whites, my grandmother always said, 'You have seen nothing yet. It was worse in Paul Kruger's time. Then the Boers protected us from the British. They protected us with the gun and the word of God. The white man was your god and you couldn't think anything different.'

She never got tired of telling us about 'Paul Kruger's time' and how hard things were. She told us about her husband, Titus, the shoe repairer who took his family from place to place looking for a better life. 'At least you have Marabastad to live in,' she said.

Aunt Dora never thought about the past and she didn't think about the future either. She tried hard to deal with the difficulties of the present. I often sat on the back veranda and watched my grandmother and Aunt Dora doing the white people's washing. They stood there for hours, talking. Sometimes they lifted up their aprons to wipe the sweat from their faces. Aunt Dora was in her thirties and she was a big woman with strong thick arms. When she lost her temper, she threw the soap and rarely missed the person she was aiming at.

A number of things made Aunt Dora lose her temper. For example, she hated it when the tea or sugar ran out and I had to ask her for money. I was careful to ask her for it at the right time. It was good to ask her when she had a visitor. It was also good to ask her when she was eating meat because she loved meat. She sometimes bought a beefsteak for herself and cooked it over the brazier in the backyard. When she was eating steak, she gave me sixpence without shouting at me.

Aunt Dora and my mother were very different. If Aunt Dora didn't like something, she went into the backyard and shouted about it. When my mother was upset with Aunt Dora, she came and told my grandmother about it. Everyone in the family looked up to[61] my mother because she was patient and wise and she always helped people with money and advice.

'She's too good for this world,' Aunt Dora said.

We went to Abdool's shop most often. Abdool, like the other shopkeepers, gave customers a small book to keep. He rubber-stamped[62] the page every time we spent sixpence. When the book was full with about two hundred stamps, he gave us two cups and saucers. At Christmas, even if the book wasn't full, he gave us two cups and saucers and two mugs as a present. Once I bought ten shillings' worth of groceries but Abdool wouldn't stamp the book for the whole amount. He said that if we bought so much the book would fill up too soon.

When Aunt Dora heard this, she took me and the book back to the shop immediately to make Abdool change his mind.

'Stamp the book for the ten shillings I spent with you

at once!' my aunt shouted as she banged the book on the shop counter. Aunt Dora spoke in very good English to the shopkeeper. 'You said he stamped for five shillings only, eh?' she said to me, pulling me nearer to the counter. I nodded my head.

'No-no-no! Ten shillings is too much,' cried Abdool.

'Abdool, stamp this book before I cause a big smash-up!' said Aunt Dora.

'Why are you causing so much trouble? Why? All the time you make trouble,' he replied.

'The trouble comes from you. You aren't honest,' she said bitterly. 'Look at my hands. I work hard for my money.'

'I also work for me and my children,' cried Abdool.

'Stamp that book, I say, Coolie! Have you come from India to make money from us, eh?' shouted Aunt Dora.

'If I'm a Coolie, you're a Kaffir yourself,' he replied.

In a moment, Aunt Dora had pushed me away from the counter and leant over it to take hold of Abdool's collar. He was much smaller than her. Aunt Dora put one knee up on the counter.

'Come outside and I'll deal with you, Coolie,' she kept saying, and Abdool kept saying, 'Let go, let go, you Kaffir bitch[63].'

Aunt Dora pulled herself up onto the counter and fell off onto the other side. She quickly got up and pushed Abdool out of the shop. My heart was beating fast both from fear and from admiration of Aunt Dora. I quickly picked up the book and went outside. I was thinking of the two cups and saucers the book would be worth if Aunt Dora won her fight. A crowd of people gathered round the two of them. Some were shouting at my aunt and some were cheering. All of them were enjoying the fight very much. Abdool was still shouting at Aunt Dora to let go of him. All of Abdool's family appeared from the rooms at the back of the shop, talking all the time in their own language.

'Abdool, stamp this book before I cause a big smash-up!'

Aunt Dora crashed her head a few times on Abdool's face. Blood came from his mouth and then they fell over on the ground. They rolled down from the veranda and onto the dusty street and my aunt shouted at him, 'Are you going to stamp the book, Abdool?'

He said a few words, and my aunt stopped fighting and got up. His family helped him to stand up and he went back into the shop. Aunt Dora followed him in, pulling her blouse, which was badly torn, to cover herself.

The book was stamped and we nearly got enough stamps to get two cups and saucers that day. My grandmother said it was a good thing her husband, Titus, Aunt Dora's father, was dead. If he had been alive, he would have beaten her. He had beaten her several times when she was a girl. Grandmother prayed for Aunt Dora and the people in the location said it was typical of Dora of Second Avenue to beat up a man.

10

Rebone and Dinku Dikae

'Are you coming to my house tonight?' asked Rebone.
'Yes,' I said.

We walked down Barber Street at the end of a school day.

'That new teacher gives us too many notes,' she said.

'Well, we aren't in Standard Five anymore,' I replied.

'Well, if he kills us with too much work, there won't be a Standard Six,' she said.

'I don't mind notes,' I replied. 'I feel more and more grown up with more and more books to carry.'

'Look there!' she said suddenly.

'What?' I asked.

'Look, over there. There's my father. Someone's stopped him. Let's go and see,' she said.

A white man in a black uniform was talking to Rebone's father and examining his horse. He was looking in the horse's mane, under its tail, at its hoofs.

'It's not a policeman, Pa,' I heard Rebone say in a quiet hiss. 'It's not a policeman.'

Dinku Dikae didn't seem to hear her. I had never seen a man look so frightened. He trembled[64] and followed the man around without saying a word.

'Don't be afraid, Pa,' she hissed. 'He's a health inspector, not a policeman.'

When the white man left, saying, 'All right' in a harsh[65] voice, Dinku Dikae held onto the horse tightly. He looked as if he was going to fall down.

'Let's go, Pa,' said Rebone. She knew that he wouldn't be able to work for the rest of the day.

It was true that we were all afraid of the police with their handcuffs[66], their truncheons[67], their heavy boots and their shining badges. Most of the policemen we saw were Zulus who were tall, heavy men; the white police only came to deal with beer and tax and pass raids. But I wondered why a big man like Dinku Dikae was more afraid of the police than the rest of us were.

I went to do school work with Rebone at her house as usual but her father was silent and Rebone was sad.

'I look after my horse well,' Dinku Dikae said. 'I look after him very well. What does the white man want now? Police, police, police, all the time there are police. I came here for peace, but I can't find any peace.'

'He's *not* a policeman, Pa,' Rebone said.

'When a white man looks for a fault, he wants to take you to the police,' he replied. He stopped talking and looked at me. I understood that he wanted me to listen to him. And then he told me his story.

'We lived in Prospect Township in the Golden City, Ezekiel. There were three of us: me, Rebone and her mother. In Prospect you have to sell beer or work for a white man and I didn't want to work for a white man. God gave me brains so I could work for myself and I made enough money for us all. Then Rebone's mother got pregnant and she became ill. I ran to a hospital for a doctor but I had to come home without one. As God is my witness[68], I had to come home and watch Rebone's mother and the baby die. I thought I had seen enough terrible things, but then the government of Johannesburg decided to destroy Prospect and build factories there. The people refused to move and the police came in again and again. We asked the government to stop but they sent the police again. We cried with misery[69] and we cried with anger and some of us threw stones at the police. Then a large number of them came with guns and shot at us. A boy came out of the house next to ours, crying for help, and a policeman shot and killed him. As

God is my witness, while Rebone and I were looking out of our window, he shot the boy and killed him.'

Dinku Dikae held up his big hands in the air and he looked both very strong and very helpless.

'I wanted to take Rebone away from Prospect so she could grow up in peace. I can't go back home to Zeerust in the west of the country because the white man has taken all the good land. But now it is hard here because people don't have much money and they don't buy much anymore.'

It was true, fewer people were buying the vegetables Dinku Dikae sold. Rebone left school in January of 1934 in the middle of Standard Six, the last primary school year. She had to help her father. Rebone and I were both sixteen years old.

'Your father tells me that you were at the Columbia Dance Hall last night,' I said to Rebone one Sunday morning.

'Why did he tell you that?' she asked angrily. 'What were *you* doing there the other night?'

'I just went to look,' I said.

'I had a better reason,' she replied. 'I went to dance.'

'Dance?' I repeated, amazed.

'Don't girls dance to Marabi jazz?' she answered, as if it was normal.

'But you danced at the Columbia. Didn't your father beat you for doing that?'

'He couldn't catch me,' she said. We both laughed.

People talked all over Marabastad about Rebone going to the Columbia. They were shocked. Rebone worked hard to help her father but she often went to the Columbia. She tried to get me to go but I was afraid. I wasn't just afraid of my grandmother, I was afraid of going with Rebone. I dreamt about it because I wanted to go and I wanted to dance with her. I loved her more and more because she had the strength to go and I didn't. I stopped going to visit her at home. I didn't plan this, it just happened. So, when Ma-Lebona and Rebone

54

had an argument, I heard about it from my friend Moloi. Ma-Lebona met Rebone at the water tap and Moloi was there. He told me what they said.

'My child,' Ma-Lebona said to her, 'daughter of Dinku Dikae, why don't you go back to school?'

'Why?' asked Rebone. She was looking at the old lady like a cat looks at a dog.

'Because you're too young for the whole of Marabastad to say evil things about you. They say evil things because you go to the Columbia Dance Hall.'

'Why don't you talk like this to your own children, old mother?' replied Rebone. 'You couldn't keep two daughters-in-law, so why are you giving me advice?'

'Ao! My own children never spoke to me like this,' cried Ma-Lebona. 'You're insulting me and I'll speak to your father about it.'

'Yes you will, because you want him to marry you,' replied Rebone.

'Ao, ao, ao, ao,' cried the old lady, clapping her hands together. 'You mustn't say that, child!'

Moloi continued the story, 'And then Rebone dipped a small cup into her tin of water and splashed water on the old lady's face.'

'What did Ma-Lebona say?' I asked.

'She didn't say anything. She turned round and left, wiping her face with her apron.'

I was amazed that Ma-Lebona just turned round and left. This was Ma-Lebona who told everybody what to do. People in Marabastad were amazed too – Rebone had splashed water on Ma-Lebona's face – yes, they could understand that. But they couldn't believe that Ma-Lebona had done nothing.

'That little wasp!' Ma-Lebona kept hissing when she told my grandmother and Aunt Dora about it. 'That little wasp will be in trouble soon. She'll have a baby or she'll drive poor Dinku Dikae mad.'

I met Rebone often after that but neither of us mentioned Ma-Lebona. Soon, Rebone found a boyfriend at the Columbia whose name was Fanyan. He was a member of the XY Ranch gang from Tenth Avenue. I hated him and I was pleased to hear stories about how evil he was. I heard that Dinku Dikae hated Fanyan too and beat Rebone for seeing him. But I couldn't blame Rebone for finding a boyfriend.

11

St Peter's School

At primary school, I gained a first-class pass in my examinations at the end of Standard Six. My class teacher gave me a book of adventure stories for boys as a prize. It was the end of primary school and my family had to decide what I would do next. Two of my uncles had gone to higher education institutions. One of them had gone to St Peter's Secondary School, which was in Rosettenville, a white suburb south of Johannesburg. It was a boys' school which was run by a religious community – the Community of the Resurrection. The Community also ran a girls' school – St Agnes's – in the same place. My uncle suggested to my mother that she should send me to St Peter's School if she could afford it. She earned £3 a month as a servant and the fees were £15 a year. She also had to pay fees and buy books for my younger brother and sister who were still at primary school. But she decided to send me to secondary school.

'You'll come back and you'll be able to look after yourself and your brother and sister,' she said.

When I first arrived in mid-January 1935, I was awed[70] by the size of the school buildings which were very large and built of brick. I felt lost, even though I was with two or three boys from my primary school. Most of the boys boarded at the school and there were just a few who lived at home and came every day. I didn't like the idea of sleeping in a dormitory with a lot of other boys. There were six dormitories in which about two hundred boys slept. Mine was called Livingstone. But the classrooms were much better than the classrooms in our Marabastad school and the science laboratory was well equipped. The boys took turns at serving food to other students in the dining-hall and collecting milk from the farm half a mile away. We also had to clean the dormitories and classrooms and keep the grounds of the school tidy. Every Monday a teacher and the head prefect[71] checked that we had done our washing and ironing correctly.

I had no idea what secondary school education was for, so for a long time I was confused. Mathematics, chemistry and physics were new to me. 'You'll never be able to do mathematics, my boy,' the African mathematics master often said. But I was the best in our class at English and Latin and I did well in the mid-year and end-of-year tests.

For the first time in my life, when I was at St Peter's, I started to understand the white man's behaviour and aims. At school, the white and the African students and teachers all got on well together. But no one ever told us how we should behave towards white authority and white people outside school. I slowly realized how I hated the white man outside of the walls of the school.

There was a double-decker bus service for Europeans from Rosettenville to the centre of Johannesburg. Coloured people were allowed to sit in a corner of the upper deck and a few conductors[72] allowed Africans to sit there as well. But mostly we walked to the city or used a tram service for Africans which did not run very often. One Saturday afternoon, a friend and I were returning to school from the city and we got on a bus. We had already left the city centre when the conductor came.

'What do you want here?' he asked.

'We're going to school,' I said.

'This is not for Kaffirs,' the conductor said.

'We're Coloureds,' said my friend.

'You're as black as Kaffirs and you tell me you're Coloureds!' said the conductor. None of the white people turned round and I saw their hard backs and hard red necks.

'Get off!' said the conductor, pressing a button near the

door. The bus stopped and we had to walk four miles back to school.

One Sunday afternoon, I was walking with two friends near the school. We were on a school outing and we were walking on the road when two whites on a motorcycle came straight at us from the opposite direction. We had to jump onto the pavement and I shouted at them, without thinking, 'Get out of our way, you Boers!'

They complained to the head prefect. We were taken to the headmaster. 'Do you want us to be thrown out of this place by the Europeans?' he asked us. 'If you swear at Europeans, they *will* throw us out.'

In Rosettenville, I gradually started to put my experience of life in Pretoria into the context[73] of life in South Africa. St Peter's boys and St Agnes's girls were allowed complete freedom to debate[74] any kind of subject. One of the teachers invited several white men to come and talk to us about various topics. One of the bigger senior boys, Zephania Mothopeng, was the 'firebrand[75]' of the school. He often said that white rule and British imperialism in Africa would end. As I listened, I thought about my life. I thought about poverty and my mother's acceptance of her life. I thought about Aunt Dora's toughness and about my grandmother, whose ways linked past and present. I thought about police raids, the ten-to-ten curfew bell and embarrassing meetings with whites. But I only became more confused as I tried hard to understand everything.

In 1935, my first year at St Peter's, I had two Coloured friends. Thomas had an African father and a Coloured mother and he did not behave in the arrogant way most Johannesburg Coloureds did. He was a loveable and intelligent friend. The other Coloured friend was Peter Abrahams, who is now a well-known writer. He thought it would be wonderful if all the black people in the world came back to Africa. He wrote poetry in his exercise books and gave it to us to read. I admired his poetry because he was trying to write poems like the ones in our school books. I remember now how angry and unhappy his poetry was. Peter made friends with a white Jewish couple who lived near the school and they often came to the school to see him. We were confused by this and filled with awe. 'He has white friends, you know,' the boys said. Peter often told me that he wanted to show the white man that he was equal to him. That frightened me a bit at that time.

When the holidays came, I felt strange in the streets of Pretoria after a few months at St Peter's. Life at home seemed very harsh. But I still helped with the cleaning and cooking and carrying washing until I left secondary school.

'Where have you been all these months?' asked Ma-Bottles when I first went back to collect washing from her.

'At school in Johannesburg, Madam,' I answered.

'College?' she asked.

'Yes, Madam,' I said.

She just made a rude noise and didn't ask anything else.

Rebone was still continuing her love affair with Fanyan but not very seriously. Her father's business had started to do well again so she had gone back to school to finish Standard Six.

The year 1936 passed quietly for me. We didn't go to school on the day King George V died. We tried to go to the Empire Exhibition which celebrated the fiftieth anniversary – the golden jubilee – of Johannesburg. But we were pushed out of the exhibition by whites. I still worked hard at mathematics and actually took an examination in it and I remained top of my class.

Three important things happened in 1937, in the final year of the Junior Certificate course. Firstly, it was the year King George VI was crowned in Britain and there was a public holiday. We were offered food and cold drinks in cups with a picture of the King on them but we decided to boycott[76] the refreshments and smash the cups. We said we couldn't accept them because we were not going to get the things we wanted. We wanted more schools, more opportunities to go to university, better pay for our parents and better houses. The school authorities took no notice of us but we tried to feel triumphant[77].

Secondly, I made love to a girl called Maria Louw at St Agnes's one Sunday morning, the day we could visit the girls' school. I didn't feel as triumphant as I expected to. I felt guilty. Something my mother said was on my mind day and night. 'You must never fail an examination, my child.' And so two weeks later I went to St Agnes's feeling very determined.

'I'm going to leave you,' I said to Maria.

'Why? Why?' she cried.

'I'm busy.'

'Busy people love each other,' she said. I shook my head.

'Have I done anything wrong?' she asked. I felt awful – I hated the thought of seeing her sad face all the time.

'No, you've done nothing wrong,' I said.

'Why are you leaving me then?' she asked.

'I've got too much work.' I felt like I was going to scream and run away.

'You've got another girl!' she said. I couldn't answer and I just sat beside her. We were quiet for a long time.

'Well, I must go now. Goodbye,' I said. The hurt look on her sweet face comes back into my mind very often.

The third thing that happened shortly after this was that I had a nervous breakdown[78] and I couldn't take the half-yearly tests. I knew that if I failed, my mother couldn't afford to pay the fees for me to study for the whole year again. But I recovered and I started working well again. In the 1937 final examinations I got a first-class pass. Three other boys, including my friend Thomas, did too. I had the certificate framed and hung it up on the wall.

When we registered for the examination, Thomas gave his surname as 'Bennet', not his real African name. He said that if his certificate was in his real name, he wouldn't be allowed into the Coloured and Indian Normal College for teacher training. If he had to go to an African college, he would get a very low salary when he became a teacher. This was true. A Coloured or an Indian teacher would get four times the salary of an African teacher with the same qualifications. I didn't feel disappointed when Thomas did that, but I didn't want to do the same thing. In fact, I didn't feel as if I could do such a thing.

12

Trouble with Whites

I now had a first-class Junior Certificate. My mother and my uncle who had been at St Peter's discussed what I should do next. My uncle suggested teacher training.

'When he's a teacher he can look after himself,' he said. 'The best school is the one I've been attending, Adams College in Natal. And as you've always helped me, Sister, I'll show you my thanks by paying his train fare. But it's too late to apply for 1938 so he'll have to work until next January. And he can save money to buy his clothing.'

'Do you want to go to Adams, Eseki?' they asked.

I didn't know what I wanted to do, but I said yes. So it was decided that I would go to Adams College in 1939.

I looked for a job in Pretoria and hated every moment of the embarrassing process. At last I got a job as a messenger in a lawyer's office. The owner was a tall, serious-looking man. I tried to say good morning to him a few times but he never answered so I stopped trying. I trembled all the time while I cleaned his inkpots and the glass on his desk and our eyes never met.

I ran up and down the stairs in buildings where blacks weren't allowed to use the lifts. I made tea and ran errands[79] for white girls who seemed to think up things for me to do when they saw me. Every instruction they gave to me ended in the words 'you hear?' I got £1 a week for putting up with[80] this and my mother kept all the money for me. She allowed me a shilling a week to go to the movies.

I had plenty of trouble with whites and their arrogant way of behaving. They said 'Yes, John?' or 'Yes, Jim?' to me and 'What do you want, boy?' I sometimes answered rudely and white boys chased me and beat me 'to put the Kaffir in his place [p]'. I took offence[81] if I thought a white person had said anything about me. I sometimes woke up during the night remembering an unpleasant experience with whites during the day. I remembered the girl who phoned someone and said, 'Mr Smith, here's the Kaffir with the documents.' I remembered the old man who came up to me in the street and said, 'Jim, where's the post office?' I remembered the post office clerk who shouted, 'If you Kaffirs don't stand straight in a line, I won't serve you.' I remembered all these insults as I lay awake at night. I kept imagining how I should have answered them.

Pretoria, like a lot of the big towns, was full of political activity. The 'Hertzog Bills' became law at that time and they were a cause of bitterness amongst the Africans. We were given a separate voters' roll[82], just for blacks. We could only vote for white representatives[83] in Parliament and for the Native Representative Council (NRC), a black Parliament outside the main Parliament. Residential segregation was enforced[84] by law so a black man could only buy land in certain areas. He couldn't buy land from a white man and the white man couldn't buy land from a black man. Some of the important Africans in politics decided to support the NRC and some didn't. In 1938, while I was working in Pretoria, it was usual for people to go on Sundays to the political meetings of the African National Congress (ANC), which represented the views of many black South Africans. I attended some because I was curious but I never really understood what was happening.

———

One Sunday night at Rebone's house, I told her how much I loved her but she laughed, 'You can't be serious, Es'ki!'

'How can I show you that I'm serious?' I asked.

'Let's not be serious,' she replied.

'But I am,' I said.

She laughed. I could tell by the way she laughed that she

just thought of me as a friend. I couldn't help feeling annoyed.

'What about Fanyan?' she asked suddenly.

'Now you're not being serious,' I replied.

'Let's forget the subject,' she said. 'Tell me what's on at the Empire.'

The Empire was the cinema which was once called The Star Picture Palace. I told her I didn't dare take her to the cinema if she was still going out with Fanyan and I went home.

Three hours later, Rebone suddenly appeared at my home and went straight to my grandmother.

'He's killed him,' she said. 'He's killed the policeman.'

'Who?' asked Aunt Dora.

'Papa. Papa has killed a white man. A white policeman. Dead. He's lying dead on the floor,' Rebone said.

'Let's go, child,' said my grandmother, putting her black shawl round her shoulders. Aunt Dora and two uncles followed her out of the house.

Rebone told me all about it the next day, and she later gave exactly the same evidence in court at her father's trial.

This is what she told me: They were both asleep, her father on one side of the room and her on the other. Her father was very tired and was sleeping like a dead man. He hadn't eaten his meal because he was so tired and she had left it on the table for him. She suddenly woke up when she heard a knock on the door.

She called, 'Who's that?' and she heard a voice shout, 'Open up, Kaffir.'

She knew it must be a white man and it must be a policeman so she woke her father. She told him that a white policeman was at the door. He sat up in bed and rubbed his eyes and said, 'What?' and she said, 'It's a policeman. It's a white policeman.'

Then she went to the door and told the man that her father was coming to open it. She looked at Dinku Dikae and his face was angry. He was trembling as he always trembled when he saw a policeman. He opened the door and the white man came in alone, with a big shining badge on his hat. 'Why did you leave me outside for so long?' he said. 'What are you hiding, Kaffir?'

'Nothing,' Dinku Dikae said and he didn't speak another word.

'You're lying. You're lying through your big black mouth. Or you were under the blankets with her?' said the policeman.

He pointed at Rebone when he said this and she saw that her father stopped trembling then. The white man went to her father's bed and pulled off the mattress and sheets. She didn't know what he was looking for. He cursed and cursed and then he came to Rebone's bed.

As he bent over the bed, her father took the breadknife from the table and went across the room to him. The white man looked up at Dinku Dikae who pushed the knife deep into the side of his neck. He left the knife there and the white man fell to the floor. Then Dinku Dikae said, 'I'll never be afraid of a policeman again, as God is my witness.'

Dinku Dikae had told Rebone to tell the whole truth and she did this in the witness box in court. It was the first time I had ever seen her cry. All Dinku Dikae said in his defence was, 'I killed him because he insulted me and my family.' He told the court what the policeman had said to him and he refused to answer any other questions.

Dinku Dikae was sentenced to death and I remember how strong he looked as he was led out of the court. I saw him again a few days before I left Pretoria and he looked stronger and more confident than I had ever seen him. The day that he was hanged, there was sadness everywhere, not only in Marabastad, but in Bantule, Cape Location and in Lady Selbourne.

Just before I left to go to college in Natal, Fanyan disappeared. Rebone went to Kilnerton Teacher Training Institution, a Methodist college near Pretoria. Her father had left her a lot of money so she could afford to go there. We wrote to each other often and often she told me not to write with such passion!

13

Adams College and Beyond

One day in early 1939, I arrived at Amanzimtoti, which means 'sweet waters', by taxi. It was twenty-two miles from the city of Durban. Then I walked a few hundred yards and entered a new world – Adams College. About four hundred men and women studied there, twice the number studying at St Peter's and St Agnes's. This college, run by the American Board of Missions, covered a wide area. We travelled long distances between Jubilee, the men's hostel where I lived, and the classrooms and dining-hall. When the students left Jubilee, they were like stampeding[85] animals. I soon got used to hearing Zulu war songs and the big, tall, bony people who were so different from 'up-country' people like me. When I left Adams College, I remembered that there were two types of tribalism[86] in Natal, the English and the Zulu. To the Zulus we were foreigners in their country.

The college buildings were big and built of stone. Lots of trees and plants grew around them and the floors of the dormitories were always dusty. Those of us from St Peter's soon realized that we would not be able to keep things clean like we had at our last school.

There was a strange collection of teachers at Adams. Dr Edgar Brookes was the principal. Brookes was also a senator[87] representing Natal Africans in the South African Parliament. He was away in Cape Town at Parliament from January to June each year. While he was away, a small German man called Dr Brueckner acted as principal. Many of the white teachers looked tired and bored. There were also very large African teachers and severe-looking white missionaries who were always telling us how lucky we were to get an education.

I walked a few hundred yards and entered a new world.

Perhaps we were lucky. But we were not allowed to say what we thought like we were at St Peter's. At Adams College, and at a great number of schools, certain political journals were banned and topics for school debates were controlled. In fact, political discussions were not allowed. If the authorities did not like what students did or said, they expelled[88] them from the college and no other college would take them. In 1940, there were student strikes[89], particularly at Fort Hare University College. There was a group of young men who were very politically active. Later some of them formed the Youth League of the ANC or became part of the All-African Convention (AAC). And, while the Second World War was happening around the world, students in South Africa were burning down school buildings.

I did not think much about politics because I concentrated on my studies. I always told myself that I mustn't fail my exams. Then something wonderful happened. I was told that the Natal Provincial Education Department had given me a scholarship to cover my fees for my two years at Adams College. I could pay my mother back the £22 she had paid for me already. After I wrote to her about this, she sent me a letter which was covered with tears. With £15 of the money, she paid to divorce my father, nine years after he had left her.

———

At the end of 1940, Reverend Arthur William Blaxall, the principal of an institute for blind people, wrote to the principal of Adams College. He asked him to recommend a student who was leaving and wanted to work as a clerk. The institute was called Ezenzeleni and it was the only institute for blind people in the Transvaal, the Orange Free State and Natal. They asked me and I took the job. I don't know why I did as I had enjoyed my teacher training. But in January 1941, Mr Blaxall collected me from Roodepoort Station, twelve miles from Johannesburg, and took me to Ezenzeleni.

I learnt how to use a typewriter so I could do the clerical work. I also learnt how to drive a car so I could deliver things made by the blind people to Johannesburg and nearby towns. Twice a week, I taught blind men how to type and enjoyed doing this very much. I was paid £6.10s per month, the same amount as a teacher earned. One Sunday a month I took the blind men and women to church. For several years I had attended the Anglican Church and I continued to do this. I didn't think why I was doing it. And that year, I began to study as an external student for the Matriculation Certificate. It was hard to pay for books, to send money to my mother and to buy clothes. So I didn't save any money in the four and a half years that I worked at Ezenzeleni.

In 1942, I took six subjects in the examinations for the Joint Matriculation Board of the University of South Africa. The university was for Europeans and also for non-whites as external students. I was unhappy when I got a third class pass, but the superintendent arranged for my pay to go up to £10 per month with an extra £2 for the cost of living. I still couldn't save any money though. My sister and brother were both at a high school in Pretoria, and the rest of my family needed more and more money too. The war was making poverty even worse.

During the time I was working at Ezenzeleni, the Pretoria city government decided to move the location of Marabastad. This had happened before with other locations. Marabastad was moved to Atteridgeville, nine miles away from Pretoria. People who rented their houses were happy to move away from the squalor[90] of Marabastad. They got three-roomed houses with electric lighting, a small coal stove and a fenced yard. People who owned their houses in Marabastad were unhappy because the compensation[91] was very low. And they were not allowed to own houses in the new location. They had to rent them. People were also unhappy because they had to travel further to and from work.

Grandmother was resigned to the change. 'The white man's law makes things happen. The white man is our god now,' she said. 'But it will be nice to live and die in a new house. And wherever I live I want to be buried beside my husband, Titus. I'm just happy to know that I have sent you all to school and you can all look after yourselves.'

My grandmother's youngest son had saved enough money to buy a house in the African township of Lady Selbourne and he took her to live with him. Aunt Dora and her family also bought a house and land in the same township.

My mother left her job as a servant, moved to Atteridgeville and looked after my brother and sister. She was getting older and thinner now and she wasn't as strong as she once was. She took a job at the mint[92] in the city and travelled there each day. She was very upset when my brother and sister decided they didn't want to go to high school anymore. They knew that I couldn't afford to send them to training colleges so they said there was no point in staying at school. I felt terribly sorry that I couldn't repay my mother and family for everything they had done for me. I visited often and spent all my holidays in Pretoria.

I often visited Rebone during the holidays. We talked about the old days when we were at school. I asked her again if she found it impossible to love me in the way I loved her.

'We're still like brother and sister, Es'ki,' she said. 'We grew up together, we know each other too well. How can we be lovers?'

When I was back at Ezenzeleni I heard that Rebone was going out with an Indian doctor. I was told that everyone in Pretoria was talking about it. It was very unconventional[93] for an African to go out with an Indian. I was jealous. When I saw him I knew that he was unconventional – he looked like a pirate with a dark shining moustache and big, dark eyes. A few months after they started going out together, he was killed in a car accident. Rebone, who was with him, was nearly killed too.

I had to return urgently to Pretoria from Ezenzeleni in the autumn of 1943 because my mother had had a stroke[94]. She was in hospital when I got there and the doctors said she had diabetes[95]. She said that she had been feeling ill for a long time but she hadn't wanted to stop work. Now she had to stop work and learn to inject herself with medicine.

Back at Ezenzeleni, not long after this, I met a young woman called Rebecca. She was one of a group of students who came from a teacher training institute to sing for the blind people. We got on well together and soon I went to Sophiatown to visit her. Her father had died and she lived with her mother in poverty in a small tin house. Her life and mine had been very similar. I surprised myself because very soon Rebecca and I decided that we belonged together. And soon after that, I was surprised again by a very long letter from Rebone. She told me how passionately she loved me and that she always had when we were school friends. I thought about this. I knew that I couldn't forget about Rebecca. I didn't want to forget about Rebecca. But I also knew it would be hard to forget Rebone.

When I met Rebone later, she said, 'I suppose you've found somebody better than me, haven't you?' and I think that she was probably right. Rebecca loved me as much as I loved her. But I never blamed Rebone and I remember her always. She married a teacher and I think she was quite happy.

And I was happy at Ezenzeleni. My time there gave me a chance to think about my life. Some of the blind people had been very poor like me and they had made good lives for themselves. I learnt to see that my life was just one part of all the suffering of non-white people in South Africa. In June 1945, however, I decided that it was time for me to leave Ezenzeleni. I felt it was time to move somewhere else. I got a job at Orlando High School in the big township of Orlando, Johannesburg, as a teacher of Afrikaans and English.

Rebecca and I decided to get married on 29th August 1945. My mother was very pleased and said she was the happiest woman in the world. She sent out invitations and started organizing the wedding feast. There were going to be two feasts. The first one would be at the bride's home and the second one would be at my mother's home. I went to see my mother to get some things for our new home in Orlando and found that she was ill in bed.

She said, 'I feel very, very tired, as if I've been walking for miles and miles.'

A week later, I had a telephone call to say that she had died in my grandmother's arms. She was forty-five years old. I was so sad that she died just before I got married. Now I couldn't bring Rebecca into her life.

14

Married

Rebecca's family wanted a bride-price[96] of £60 and wouldn't change their minds. Rebecca and I both hated this but we had no choice – I had to earn the money. Arthur Blaxall had given me an extra clerical job and after six months I had earned enough to pay the £60. So on 29th August 1945 we were married in Sophiatown. There were big crowds of people at the wedding. Aunt Dora, my grandmother, my three uncles, my brother and sister and a few other close relatives came. We were married in the African Methodist Episcopal Church and afterwards there was happiness and dancing. But for a while, I couldn't enjoy myself. I felt lonely and sad because my mother wasn't there. At last, at the party in the evening, I began to feel better and danced through the night with my friends and relatives.

First Rebecca and I lived in a small, old house near the school in Orlando and later we lived in a new one with four quite big rooms. In the new house we had our own water tap and the rent was £2.10s. The house was on a hill, and below us I could see Shanty Town, which was a poor, miserable place. Its poverty reminded me of Second Avenue and reminded me all the time of the hard lives of African people. In 1947, I decided not to go to church anymore because a big change was happening inside me. I thought about the white press, the white radio, the white Parliament, the white employers, the white church and about the way the non-white people were treated. And I no longer accepted these things as normal.

At the same time, I loved teaching and I loved the other activities which I introduced into the school – boxing and drama. I directed and acted in several short plays. We even gave performances to multi-racial audiences. There was no law against it at that time. But the authorities wanted the whites and non-whites each 'to develop along our own lines' and multi-racial audiences became more and more unusual.

I had started writing poetry and short stories in the early 1940s at Ezenzeleni. In 1945, I had decided to send ten of my short stories to a publisher, the African Bookman, in Cape Town. The publisher wrote back to me saying they wanted to publish five of the stories. In 1947, copies of my first book were sent to me. It was a lovely little book with illustrations, called *Man Must Live*. It was a wonderful experience to see my work in print for the first time.

The white press were mostly negative in their reviews. The Cape Town magazine *Guardian*, said, 'He has forgotten he is an African … his characters never complain about the pass laws or the arrogance of the white man … the writer should look at his own people to get his ideas.' I hated to read this. I knew it was true, but I was angry because the words were written by a white man. A white man had never had to carry a pass and experience all the terrible things Africans experienced.

In 1949, four years after starting work at the high school, I got a BA degree as an external student at the University of South Africa in English, Psychology and Native Administration. I also took a degree course in Afrikaans. My salary went up to £42 a month and Rebecca and I felt we were almost rich. And now we had a son, Anthony.

I became a member of the local teachers' association and was elected secretary in the winter of 1950. At the annual conference of the Transvaal African Teachers, I spoke about the 'Code of Syllabuses[97] in Native Primary Schools'. I said that it was a code for creating slaves and I also complained about the textbooks used in African schools. I gave the example of Afrikaans grammar books with sentences in them like: *The Kaffir has stolen a knife* or *That is a lazy Kaffir*. There were also history books which praised white rule. Non-whites were shown as stupid.

I was in this rebellious state of mind[98] when the report 'Commission on Bantu Education' was published. It said that the present education system should be changed because it cut off the native students from their own 'Bantu Culture'. And the report suggested a completely new basis for African education. The Bantu Education Act which followed it in 1955 was actually a tool of oppression which enforced the *status quo*[99]. It was clear that Africans were going to be treated like slaves in their own country forever.

When the report first appeared, I campaigned against it along with Zephania Mothopeng, who was editor of the teachers' journal, and Isaac Matlare. We taught in the same high school and Zeph was still the same firebrand he had been at St Peter's. The principal of Orlando High School disagreed with our actions and supported the ideas in the report. 'You have children to feed, gentlemen,' he said to us. 'And you'll be without a job if you don't stop talking politics.'

In 1952, we were dismissed[100] from our teaching jobs and we were not given any reason for our dismissal. We were banned from teaching. We would not be allowed to teach anywhere in South Africa. A number of students decided to boycott the school in order to support us and protest against our dismissal. Then we were arrested. The police said that we were making the students boycott school. We were in jail for four days before getting bail. During our trial, several students said they had been taken to a police station and forced to blame us for their actions. So we were acquitted[101], but we were described in the press as the 'rebel teachers'. I applied for a teaching post in Bechuanaland Protectorate[102], a British-controlled territory, but I was rejected. They said that they had been told that I had been dismissed 'for subversive[103] activities'. That was the first time I learnt the reason for my dismissal.

For the rest of the year, I tried to find a job. At first, I still had documents proving that I was a teacher. As a teacher, I was exempt[104] from the pass laws but I wasn't exempt from the curfew on Africans from 11.00 p.m. to 4.30 a.m. A person who had a pass had to renew it every month with a signature from his or her employer. As soon as a person stopped working for an employer, the pass was no longer valid. At last I decided I could not say I was a teacher anymore and I went to the pass office.

I had always sympathized with the people who had to have a pass but the experience was even worse than I expected. The way I was treated in the pass office was terrible. It was like being cut with a knife. I first had my photograph taken. Then I had to hand in a piece of paper at the first official's desk. This came from the Orlando superintendent to say that I lived in his location. The official then gave me the reference book – the pass – and stuck a photograph on a page. The second official had two cards on which he wrote information about me. Another photograph of me was stuck onto one of these cards and this was filed. The next official had a rubber stamp. His job was to control the number of 'natives' in an area by listing every employer and every worker. This meant that a black man's movements were controlled at all times. He rubber-stamped a page of my book, giving me permission to look for work in Johannesburg. When I found a job, my boss would have to sign his name in the book every month. Also, I would have to get another stamp saying I had permission to stay in Johannesburg as long as I worked there. The last official could decide at any time not to let me look for work in Johannesburg and send me back to Pretoria, my place of birth.

We couldn't celebrate Christmas in 1952 because we had no money. We had two children by now and Rebecca was expecting a third baby. Then I got a job in a lawyer's office as the 'second messenger'. As I could type, I often helped the white girl typist. One day I was told not to type in the office anymore. This was because it embarrassed white clients to see a black man when they entered the office.

'Take your typewriter into the room where you make the tea,' said my employer.

I worked there for three months before I was sacked and lost my £21 a month salary. I was sacked for two reasons. I had finally refused to run any more private errands for one of the typists. And in the same week I was rude to a girl in another office.

'You must come again this afternoon, boy,' she said to me.

'What makes you think I'm a boy and not a girl?' I replied angrily.

'Now, don't be rude to me!' she said.

'I seem to have come to the right school for good manners,' I replied.

'Now, you leave before I call the police,' she said.

I told her the number that every white person is supposed to know for the police, but she did nothing. I left, feeling pleased with myself. But she complained to my employer and I was sacked.

My European friends helped us when we were nearly starving but I was too proud to ask for help very often. My ex-colleague, Zeph Mothopeng, had similar experiences to me. I had paid into an unemployment insurance fund when I was teaching and I could take out £5.5s every two weeks from this fund. I went to offices in the same building as the pass office to collect the money and joined one of the many queues of black men. We held piles of papers and moved from office to office and had our papers rubber-stamped by white officials. While we waited, white men came in and shouted out jobs they were offering: 'kitchen boy, £4 a month', 'truck driver, £3 a week,' 'garden boy, sixpence a day for two days a week'. They shouted and the Africans moved around deciding which job to take.

They didn't really have any choice. They were like animals in an auction sale.

I got a part-time job as a typist in a hatmaker's shop. The shop sold clothing to Africans who worked in the suburbs. I earned £10 a month. Rebecca was an expert housewife and cook and she got us through our difficulties. She always managed everything very well.

15

Drum *Magazine*

During the second half of 1953, I worked as a typist for Arthur Blaxall. He had retired from his job as principal of Ezenzeleni and was secretary of the Christian Council of South Africa. I was paid £20 a month and he added £8 to this himself. But by the end of the year, I was feeling terrible. I wanted very much to be a teacher again. I could live with the decrease in my salary but I felt as though my honesty had been questioned. I had no way of fighting for myself.

I applied for a job in Basutoland Protectorate and in January 1954 I started work as a teacher of English and geography. For the second time in my life, I left a clerk's job with Arthur and started teaching. My friend Zeph was also teaching there and we both had to go there without our families. A report about our 'subversive activities' was sent there, but the authorities took no notice of it.

I began studying for a BA Honours degree in English because I loved studying English. For the first few months I had plenty to do, but my salary was low, lower than Arthur's £28 and life was boring. I was an urban person and I found that I couldn't be happy in the country. In August, I decided not to return to Basutoland. I was offered a job teaching Afrikaans and mathematics at my old school, St Peter's. As I was officially banned from teaching by the government, I was paid £18 a month by the school. Rebecca was terribly worried about money.

In November, I took the examination for the BA Honours degree. I almost gave up in the middle of the examinations because I was so tired. But I continued and I passed. At the end of the year, the principal of St Peter's offered to double my salary during the following year, 1955. However, it was 'discovered' by the government that the school was in an area for whites and it had to close. After the last year in the life of St Peter's, I was going to be without work again so I took a job as a journalist and literary editor of *Drum*. This was a monthly magazine published in Johannesburg.

I didn't think I was going to be a good journalist because I hated the way the press worked in South Africa. I hated the fact that there was a press for whites and a press for non-whites. I didn't like the type of stories that *Drum* thought the urban African wanted to read – crime and love stories. The editors I worked for did publish some stories about social and political evils though. I worked for *Drum* for two and a half years and had to live two different lives while I was doing so. I edited and reported during the day and I studied and wrote my own stories at night. About seven of my short stories were published in the magazine.

It was in 1955 that I finally joined the ANC. For some years, I had tried to decide whether to join the ANC or the AAC. There had been a war of words between them since 1935. The AAC seemed very theoretical and wanted only to work with groups which agreed with them on everything. This meant that the AAC was in danger of never taking any action. The ANC was prepared to take action. It would work with other groups in order to try to improve the lives of Africans. But it didn't always make the best decisions, for example about the Bantu Education Act. There were school boycotts. Some parts of the ANC leadership did not understand that boycotting schools made life more difficult for African families. These were people who needed their children to be at school while they worked. The ANC also needed to convince parents that the Act would work as a tool of oppression in the classroom. It needed to be clearer about how to fight it. But it did not always do this.

In 1956, I decided to take an MA degree as an external student at the University of South Africa and I began research for my thesis. My subject was *The Non-European Character in South African English Fiction*. I studied English literature inside and outside Africa in which non-white characters appear. Then I studied ten South African novelists, including Peter Abrahams who had been at St Peter's at the same time as me. I concluded that: 'There cannot be a healthy culture in a country when conditions keep whole communities away from each other. There cannot be a healthy culture when there is no way of communities meeting economically or socially. And the problem of a national culture is also the problem of a national literature.'

At the end of 1956, I finished my thesis and was awarded the degree with a distinction[105]. It was the first time that the Department of English of the University of South Africa had awarded a distinction for an MA degree. The degrees for Africans were given at a separate ceremony from the degrees for Europeans. White and non-white students studied the same syllabuses and did the same examinations, but apartheid meant that there could not be a ceremony for everybody. I invited white and non-white friends to the ceremony. There were two rows of seats for whites at the front of the hall but all my friends sat together. Later, when graduates[106] and guests and staff had tea, most of the whites drank from matching cups and saucers. My white guests joined the non-white ones and drank tea from cups and saucers which didn't match. Then we partied to celebrate, with our African, Coloured, Indian and European friends all mixed together. This was not the traditional way of life in South Africa but no one cared.

At the beginning of 1957, I began to feel that I should leave South Africa. I had been banned from teaching, I was bitter about this and many other things and I felt trapped by our life – I couldn't change anything. My salary at *Drum* was

£40 a month and was never going to get any higher. I couldn't concentrate on writing and I was worried about our children's education under the new system. I wanted to leave and at the same time, I also wanted to stay and fight. But I felt I needed to build up my mental and moral strength first.

Arthur Blaxall had told me about an Overseas Employment Bureau in London which found teachers to work in East and West Africa, the Sudan and other countries. I applied and was sent a list of jobs. I chose to teach in Lagos, Nigeria and a job was given to me in the CMS Grammar School. In April, I applied for a passport though I didn't believe I would get one. Many Africans like me had been refused passports recently.

16

Ticket to Nigeria

I waited for five months and then I was told I couldn't have a passport. I went to see an African minister from the Dutch Reformed Church whom I had known for a few years and asked for his advice. I learnt from him about how an African can apply for a passport. Your application goes to the Native Commissioner. He needs three copies of a character reference from a person of authority. You also have to provide a letter from your wife or other family saying that they agree to you leaving the country. Then you pay £100. The Native Commissioner sends all the papers to the Chief Native Commissioner. He sends the papers to the Native Affairs Department along with a copy of a letter of recommendation from the Native Commissioner. The Security Branch of the Criminal Investigation Department (CID) sends a report to the Native Affairs Department, which sends all the papers to the Secretary of the Interior. These people and departments can take as long as they like to do this.

The minister went straight to the CID headquarters in Pretoria. The chief of the Security Branch showed him the file on me. It started in 1950 when I became secretary of the association of teachers. It covered my articles in the press and my speeches against the Bantu Education Act and other laws. It covered angry speeches I had made at political rallies[107]. This was why my application for a passport had been refused. The chief asked the minister how they could let a man like this out of the country. But the minister argued that if they didn't let me out, I would become more and more bitter and would become a communist. The chief said: 'Call him to my office and let's hear what he has to say.'

To my surprise, the chief was a quietly spoken, cultured man. He was white, but he was human. I wondered why he was in charge of the most feared and unpopular institution in South Africa.

The chief asked if I spoke his language, Afrikaans, and from that moment we didn't speak any more English. He asked me to tell him my life history and after he had heard it all, he said that he understood my bitterness. He said that the whites had not meant to oppress us and that he personally wanted progress for the black man.

He also said, 'If it is the last thing that I do in my life, I'll save you from communism.' He said he would ask the Secretary of the Interior to let me leave. He said that after I had left, I must remember to speak well of South Africa, which had given me my education. I must remember that South Africa was doing more for its non-white population than any colonial government in Africa. Then he said that within the next two weeks, I should get my passport.

This interview took place three weeks before my flight to Nigeria which was booked for 6th September. For those three weeks, I waited in the corridors of government offices. Every time I went I was told that all of my documents were on the desk of the Secretary of the Interior. In those offices, nobody spoke to me harshly like they did in the pass office or the post office. I simply felt the indifference[108], hate and arrogance of the power of the government around me.

The minister came with me each time I went there and he gave me the message each time. 'Die groot baas is nog besig – the big boss is still busy.' He was always patient and I was amazed at how easily I could wait. I had always feared a time when I would accept my situation easily. But at last, a day before my flight to Lagos, I went to Pretoria to collect my passport.

Within the next two weeks, I should get my passport.

On 6th September, I said goodbye to my friends and to South Africa. I had waited for nine months for this day. What a day in thirty-seven years of a man's life! In December, Rebecca and our three children, Anthony, Theresa and Motswiri, joined me to begin their life with me in Lagos.

Points for Understanding

1

1 Why did Ezekiel hate school?
2 What do we learn about religion in Maupaneng from the author?
3 What do we learn about the difference between Ezekiel's mother and his grandmother?

2

1 When Ezekiel's father told him 'you will inherit everything I have,' the boy's mother laughed. Why?
2 Why had Ezekiel's mother collected her children from the country?
3 What does the smell of a primus stove often remind Ezekiel of?

3

1 Ezekiel thought that people had a greater need for privacy in Marabastad than in the village. Give an example showing why he decided this. And why did he think that people in Marabastad did not show their feelings?
2 Ezekiel tells us about his family and his home. How can we tell that his family was poor?
3 Ezekiel tells us about what the family ate. How does this tell us that his family was poor?

4

1 Why did Ezekiel's family hide beer in oil cans?
2 What did Ezekiel feel about the police?
3 What effect did the police raids have on the behaviour of the people in Marabastad?

5

1   The school in the location was better than the school in
    Maupaneng, but in one way they were similar. What was this?
2   Ezekiel made good use of his reading skills at the movies. Explain
    how he went into business.
3   Ma-Lebona said that Rebone had looked as if she had been going to
    say, 'I'll scratch your eyes out if you come near my father.' What did
    she think that Rebone thought?

6

1   What does Ezekiel tell us about Ma-Lebona that explains why her
    husbands left her?
2   Ma-Lebona's son, Joel, always obeyed his mother but this did not
    bring him happiness. Explain why.
3   How did the white people treat Ezekiel?

7

1   Ezekiel said, 'In Standard Six, I felt as if a great light had come on
    inside me.' What did he mean?
2   Why did some people think that Big Eyes was a good headmaster?
3   Who won the argument between Aunt Dora and Big Eyes? Explain.

8

1   Ezekiel's grandmother believed that the end of the world was near.
    Why did she believe this?
2   Someone in the crowd outside Boeta Lem's house said, 'If he'd
    raped a white girl, he'd have been kept in the police station. Then
    he would be hanged.' What sentence did Boeta Lem get and what
    does this say about the racial prejudice of the legal system?
3   Why did Ezekiel want to go to the Columbia Dance Hall?

9

1. Ezekiel's mother, his grandmother and his Aunt Dora all had different attitudes towards white society. Explain their differences.
2. What caused the argument between Aunt Dora and Abdool?
3. Racial prejudice was not something only the whites showed. How did the fight between Aunt Dora and Abdool show this?

10

1. Dinku Dikae had good reasons to fear the police. Explain his reasons.
2. How did Ezekiel start to feel about Rebone?
3. How did Ma-Lebona react when Rebone splashed water in her face and what was unusual about her reaction?

11

1. The racial segregation in South Africa tempted Ezekiel and his friend to be dishonest about themselves. Explain how a story in this chapter is an example of this.
2. Ma-Bottles made a rude noise when Ezekiel told her that he had been away at school. What does this suggest about her thoughts on the education of blacks?
3. Why did Ezekiel have a nervous breakdown?

12

1. Some of the white people Ezekiel worked for called him 'boy', 'Jim', or 'John'. What does this show about their attitude towards him?
2. Why did Rebone laugh when Ezekiel told her that he loved her?
3. Why did Dinku Dikae kill the white policeman?

13

1 Adams College was not as useful to Ezekiel as St Peter's. Explain why he thought this.
2 Why wasn't Ezekiel able to save any money during the years he worked at Ezenzeleni?
3 When the Marabastad location was moved to a different area, some of the people who lived there were happy, but others were not. Explain why.

14

1 Ezekiel mentioned that in their new home in Orlando, he and Rebecca had their own water tap. Why was this important to him?
2 When the government suggested that African students were cut off from their native culture, Ezekiel and his friends were not pleased. Explain their suspicions about the report and the following Education Act.
3 Why was Ezekiel sacked from his job at the lawyer's office?

15

1 Why did Ezekiel think he wasn't going to be a good journalist?
2 At the ceremony when Ezekiel received his MA degree, his friends showed their dislike of racial segregation. Explain how they did this.
3 Ezekiel said, 'Many Africans like me had been refused passports lately.' What did he mean by 'like me'?

16

1 How did the minister from the Dutch Reformed Church help Ezekiel?
2 What do we learn about the chief of the CID?
3 Ezekiel was amazed at how easy it was for him to wait for his passport without complaining. Did he think that this was a good thing?

Glossary

1 *suburb* (page 4)
an area or town near a large city but away from its centre, where
there are many houses

2 *backward* (page 4)
an old-fashioned word used for describing a child or student who is
unable to make normal progress in learning

3 *beating* – *to beat someone* (page 4)
to hit someone violently several times

4 *prejudice* (page 6)
an unreasonable opinion or feeling, especially the feeling of not
liking a particular group of people

5 *sentenced* – *to sentence someone to something* (page 7)
when a judge sentences someone, they officially state what
someone's punishment will be

6 *segregation* (page 7)
the policy of keeping people from different groups, especially
different races, separate

7 *oppress* – *to oppress someone* (page 7)
to treat people who are less powerful in an unfair and cruel way.
This kind of unfair treatment is called *oppression*.

8 *stern* (page 10)
a stern person, expression or statement is serious and severe

9 *tickled* – *to tickle someone or something* (page 10)
if something *tickles* you, it touches your skin gently and gives you a
pleasant feeling

10 *multiplication table* (page 10)
a list that shows the results of multiplying all the combinations
of two numbers between 1 and 12 together. If you *chant* a word or
phrase, you say or sing it many times. The school children have to
repeat *multiplication tables* in class.

11 *plough* – *to plough* (page 10)
to turn over the soil before putting seeds into it using a piece of
farm equipment called a *plough*. The seeds grow into *crops* – plants
grown for food on farms.

12 *fierce* (page 12)
very strong or severe and dangerous

13 **communal** (page 12)

owned or used by everyone in a group, especially a group of people who live in the same building or area

14 **veld** (page 12)

a large flat area covered with grass but with few trees

15 **vermin** (page 13)

small animals or insects that cause damage or disease. *Bug* is an informal word for insect and *lice* are a type of small insect that live on people's skin and in their hair.

16 **rags** (page 14)

clothes that are old, torn and dirty

17 **tough** (page 14)

strong and able to deal with difficult situations or pain

18 **slums** (page 15)

a poor area of a town where the houses are in very bad condition

19 **tailor** (page 16)

someone who makes clothes, especially clothes designed to fit individual customers

20 **limped** – *to limp* (page 16)

to walk with difficulty because of an injured leg or foot

21 **heir** (page 17)

someone who will *inherit* (= receive) money, property or a title when another person dies

22 **primus stove** (page 17)

a small piece of equipment that produces a flame for cooking by burning oil and that can be used outside

23 **court** (page 18)

a place where legal cases are decided, especially in front of a judge and a jury or a magistrate – a judge in a court for minor crimes. The process of examining a case in a court of law and deciding whether someone is guilty or innocent is called a *trial*.

24 **trickled** – *to trickle* (page 19)

if a liquid or a substance such as sand trickles somewhere, a small amount of it flows there slowly

25 **gossiped** – *to gossip* (page 19)

to talk about other people or about things that are not important

26 **iron** (page 19)

a hard heavy metal that is a common element. It is used for making steel and is also used in many types of machine and building structures. *Corrugated iron* has been shaped into parallel folds.

27 **swayed** – *to sway* (page 19)
   to move or swing gently from side to side
28 **veranda** (page 19)
   a covered area along the outside of a house, often enclosed by a low
   wall
29 **brazier** (page 19)
   a simple metal container with a fire in it, used outside for keeping
   people warm or for cooking. The fuel they use is *coke* – the solid
   grey substance that is left after coal is burnt.
30 **faeces** (page 19)
   solid waste from your body
31 **creeper** (page 21)
   a plant with long stems that grows along the ground, around other
   plants or up walls and fences
32 **dung** (page 21)
   solid waste from the body of a large animal such as an elephant or
   a cow
33 **mealie-meal** (page 22)
   a type of food made from *maize* – a tall plant that produces yellow
   seeds that are called *sweetcorn* when cooked and eaten
34 **worth** (page 22)
   an amount measured by the financial value that it has
35 **bastard** (page 22)
   an insulting word for an unpleasant or annoying man
36 **cursed** – *to curse someone* (page 22)
   to say offensive words about someone
37 **raid** – *to raid something* (page 25)
   to use force to enter a place suddenly in order to arrest people or
   search for something illegal. The action of entering a place in this
   way is called a *raid*. The white police often came to black people's
   houses to search for illegal beer and to control the people's passes.
   All black people had to carry a *pass* – an official document which
   gave their personal information and without which they could not
   work or go anywhere. A *pass raid* could happen at any time.
38 **cane** (page 26)
   a stick used for punishing children in schools. If you hit someone
   with a *cane*, you *cane* them.
39 **chum** (page 27)
   an old-fashioned word used for a close friend

40 **curfew** (page 28)
a law that does not allow people to go outside between a particular time in the evening and a particular time in the morning

41 **swinging** – *to swing something* (page 28)
to make something move, backwards and forwards or from one side to another, especially from a fixed point. Later in the book, Ezekiel watches white children playing in the park on *swings*. A *swing* is a seat hanging from chains or ropes that moves backwards and forwards and is used especially by children.

42 **wasp** (page 29)
a black and yellow flying insect that can sting you

43 **boasted** – *to boast* (page 31)
to proudly tell other people about what you or someone connected with you has done or can do, or about something you own, especially in order to make them admire you

44 **stubborn** (page 31)
a stubborn person is not willing to change their ideas or to consider anyone else's reasons or arguments

45 **ancestor** (page 32)
someone who is related to you who lived a long time ago

46 **arithmetic** (page 36)
the part of mathematics that involves basic calculations such as adding or multiplying numbers

47 **tattered** (page 36)
something that is *tattered* looks in very bad condition because parts of it have been torn

48 **punish** – *to punish someone* (page 38)
to make someone suffer because they have done something against the law or against the rules. The process of punishing someone, or the way of punishing them, is called *punishment*.

49 **division** (page 39)
one of the parts into which a large organization is divided

50 **poverty** (page 40)
a situation in which someone does not have enough money to pay for their basic needs

51 **insult** – *to insult someone* (page 41)
to say or do something offensive

52 **raped** – *to rape someone* (page 41)
to force someone to have sex by using violence

53 **lawyer** (page 42)
someone whose profession is to provide people with legal advice and services

54 **bailed** – *to bail someone* (page 42)
to allow someone to stay out of prison while they wait for their trial, after money has been paid as *bail*

55 **hanged** – *to hang someone* (page 42)
to kill someone by putting a rope around their neck and making them fall

56 **hard labour** (page 43)
very hard physical work that some people have to do when they are in prison as a punishment

57 **immoral** (page 43)
relating to behaviour that people think is wrong. Behaviour that people think is wrong is called *immorality*.

58 **sermon** (page 44)
a speech made by a priest or religious leader, especially as part of a religious ceremony. Someone whose job is to give sermons is called a *preacher* in some Christian churches.

59 **heathen** (page 45)
an insulting word for someone who is not a Christian or a follower of another major established religion

60 **bandoliers** (page 46)
a type of belt worn over one shoulder and across the chest with pockets to hold bullets

61 **looked up to** – *to look up to someone* (page 48)
to admire and respect someone

62 **rubber-stamped** – *to rubber stamp something* (page 48)
to use a small object with a piece of rubber on one end to print something on a piece of paper

63 **bitch** (page 49)
an insulting word for someone, especially a woman, who is rude or cruel

64 **trembled** – *to tremble* (page 52)
if your body or part of your body trembles, it shakes, usually because you are nervous, afraid or excited

65 **harsh** (page 52)
harsh sounds are unpleasant because they are not soft, gentle or smooth

66 **handcuffs** (page 53)
metal rings that a police officer puts round a prisoner's wrists to stop them from using their hands or arms

67 **truncheon** (page 53)
a short thick stick carried by a police officer as a weapon

68 **witness** (page 53)
someone who sees something happen and knows that someone is or is not telling the truth about it

69 **misery** (page 53)
the state of being extremely unhappy or uncomfortable

70 **awed** – *to be awed by someone or something* (page 57)
to feel great respect, admiration and sometimes fear for something

71 **prefect** (page 58)
in some schools, an older student who controls the activities of younger students and helps them to obey the rules

72 **conductor** (page 58)
someone on a bus or train who checks passengers' tickets and collects money

73 **context** (page 59)
the general situation in which something happens, which helps to explain it

74 **debate** – *to debate something* (page 59)
if people debate a subject, they discuss it formally before making a decision, usually by voting

75 **firebrand** (page 59)
someone who has strong feelings, especially about politics, and wants to change things or encourage other people to feel the same

76 **boycott** – *to boycott something* (page 60)
to not take part in an event, or to not buy or use something as a protest

77 **triumphant** (page 61)
very pleased or excited about a victory or success

78 **nervous breakdown** (page 61)
a mental condition in which you are so upset or unhappy that you cannot look after yourself

79 **errands** (page 63)
a small job that involves going to collect or deliver something

80 **putting up with** – *to put up with something* (page 63)
to accept someone or something unpleasant in a patient way

81 **took offence** – *to take offence* (page 64)
to feel angry and upset because of something that someone has said or done

82 **voters' roll** (page 64)
an official list of all the people in an area who have the right to vote in elections

83 **representative** (page 64)
someone who has been chosen or elected by a person or group to vote, give opinions or make decisions for them

84 **enforced** – *to enforce something* (page 64)
to make sure that a law or rule is obeyed by people

85 **stampeding** – *to stampede* (page 68)
if a group of animals or people stampede, they all start to run in a very fast uncontrolled way because they are frightened or excited

86 **tribalism** (page 68)
a way of thinking or behaving in which people are more loyal to their tribe than to their friends, their country or any other social group

87 **senator** (page 68)
someone who is a member of a senate – the more powerful part of a law-making institution that has two parts

88 **expelled** – *to expel someone* (page 70)
to force a student to leave a school permanently

89 **strike** (page 70)
a period of time during which people refuse to work, as a protest about pay or conditions of work

90 **squalor** (page 71)
dirty and unpleasant conditions that people live or work in

91 **compensation** (page 71)
money that someone receives because something bad has happened to them

92 **mint** (page 72)
the place where a country makes its coins and paper money

93 **unconventional** (page 72)
different from what most people consider to be usual or normal

94 **stroke** (page 73)
a medical condition in which blood is suddenly blocked and cannot reach the brain, or in which a blood vessel in the brain breaks, often causing a loss of the ability to speak or to move particular muscles

95 **diabetes** (page 73)
    a serious medical condition in which your body does not produce
    enough of a substance called insulin, which controls the level of
    sugar in your blood. Some people who suffer from diabetes have to
    inject themselves with insulin – put it into their body through their
    skin, using a needle.
96 **bride-price** (page 75)
    money that, in some cultures, a man gives to a woman's family
    when he marries her
97 **syllabus** (page 76)
    a list of the main subjects in a course of study
98 **state of mind** (page 77)
    the way that you are thinking and feeling at a particular time
99 **status quo** (page 77)
    the present situation, or the way that things usually are
100 **dismissed** – *to dismiss someone* (page 77)
    to force someone to leave their job. The act of making someone
    leave their job is called *dismissal*.
101 **acquitted** – *to acquit someone* (page 77)
    to state officially that someone is not guilty of the crime they were
    accused of
102 **Protectorate** (page 77)
    an area or country that is defended and controlled by a more
    powerful country
103 **subversive** (page 77)
    intended to destroy the power or influence of a government or an
    established belief
104 **exempt** (page 78)
    allowed to ignore something such as a rule, obligation or payment
105 **distinction** (page 83)
    a very high mark in an examination
106 **graduate** (page 83)
    someone who has a degree from a university
107 **rally** (page 85)
    a public meeting that a lot of people go to in order to support
    someone or something or to protest against someone or something
108 **indifference** (page 86)
    lack of interest or sympathy

Useful Phrases

she's got a cheek – *someone has got a cheek* (page 28)
used for describing someone's behaviour – *cheek* is behaviour that is rude or does not show respect, especially towards someone who is older or more important

I'll scratch your eyes out – *to scratch someone's eyes out* (page 29)
to fight or argue with someone in a very angry and cruel way

she's met her match – *to meet your match* (page 33)
to be in a situation in which your opponent is as good as you or better

it was like the dawn of a new day (page 37)
used for describing the time when something such as a new period in history begins. *Dawn* is the beginning of the day, when it begins to get light.

put the Kaffir in his place – *to put someone in their place* (page 64)
to do or say something to someone that shows them that you do not think they are important

Glossary and Useful Phrases definitions adapted from Macmillan English Dictionary 2nd Edition
© *Macmillan Publishers Limited 2007* www.macmillandictionary.com

Exercises

Background Information

Choose the correct information to complete the sentences.

1 Ezekiel mostly lived with his parents / <u>grandparents</u>.

2 He spoke <u>two</u> / three languages.

3 He didn't like studying <u>geography</u> / mathematics.

4 He studied to become a <u>journalist</u> / teacher.

5 He spent <u>a short</u> / a long time in prison.

6 The book is fictional / <u>a true story</u>.

7 The <u>black</u> / white people had all the political power at the time.

8 The <u>Coloureds</u> / Africans had the worst living conditions.

9 Apartheid laws made life <u>better</u> / worse for non-white people.

10 Ezekiel saw many <u>similarities</u> / differences between the black African tribes.

11 Nelson Mandela became president of South Africa in <u>1984</u> / 1994.

People in the Story

Write a name from the box next to the correct information below.

| Abdool   Anthony   Arthur Blaxall   Dinku Dikae   Dora |
| Hibila   Ma-Lebona   ~~Moses~~   Rebecca   Rebone |

1 ....Moses............ was Ezekiel's father.

2 .... was Ezekiel's close friend and first love at school.

3 .... was Ezekiel's neighbour in Second Avenue.

4 .... was Ezekiel's grandmother (his mother's mother).

5 .... was Ezekiel's aunt.

6 .... was the local Indian shop owner.

7 .... was Rebone's father.

8 .... was the principal of Ezenzeleni.

9 .... was Ezekiel's wife.

10 .... was Ezekiel's first son.

Places in the Story

Match the places on the left to the things Ezekiel did on the right.

1 Maupaneng	a He taught English and geography.
2 Fifth Avenue	b He worked at Ezenzeleni, an institute for the blind.
3 Second Avenue	c He went to St Peter's secondary school.
4 Rosettenville	d He lived with his father's mother.
5 Pretoria	e He had a job in a lawyer's office.
6 Amanzimtoti	f He taught Afrikaans and English.
7 The Transvaal	g He had a job in a grammar school.
8 Orlando	h He lived with his mother's mother.
9 Basutoland Protectorate	i He went to Adams College.
10 Lagos	j He lived with his mother and father.

Multiple Choice

Tick the best answer.

1 Adams College was different from St Peter's because ...
   a it only had African teachers.
   b it gave the students a lot of freedom.
   c it limited what the students could talk about. ✓

2 When he worked at Ezenzeleni, Ezekiel earned ...
   a more than a teacher.
   b the same as a teacher.
   c less than a teacher.

3 Ezekiel met Rebecca ...
   a at the institute for the blind.
   b at college.
   c in Sophiatown.

4 Ezekiel decided not to go to church anymore because ...
   a his ideas about what was normal had changed.
   b he didn't believe in a religion anymore.
   c his wife was not religious.

5 The white reviews of Ezekiel's first book were negative because ...
   a he wrote about the African experience.
   b he didn't write about the African experience.
   c they didn't understand the African experience.

6 Ezekiel decided to join the ANC because ...
   a it always did the right thing.
   b it did things to cause change.
   c it was very academic.

7 Ezekiel wanted to leave South Africa because ...
   a he couldn't find a job.
   b he couldn't change anything at that time.
   c he didn't want to fight anymore.

8 At first, Ezekiel was not given a passport because ...
   a he was a communist.
   b it got lost in the different departments.
   c a file showed his actions against the government.

Vocabulary: Anagrams

Write the letters in the correct order to make words from the story.

1	ERIH	*heir*	the person who receives money or a position after a parent dies
2	JUPERCIDE		an unfair opinion or feeling against someone or something
3	RESUC		to call someone a bad name
4	DANHCFUFS		metal hoops to tie hands together, used when someone is arrested
5	SPAW		a yellow and black insect which can sting
6	BUBTORNS		determined in a negative way
7	PEMTEX		special permission not to do or pay something
8	MONSER		a religious talk, often about how people should live
9	TERBLEM		to shake often because you are frightened
10	CENXTOT		the situation in which something happens
11	RIAD		when the police suddenly enter a building to find crimes in progress
12	TEKICL		when something touches your skin; it often makes you laugh
13	GUPLOH		to dig the land to prepare it for growing things

Words from the Story

Complete the gaps. Use each word in the box once.

> ~~cane~~   curfew   diabetes   errands   immoral
> put up with   slums   subversive   syllabus   punish

1 Teachers often used a _____ *cane* _____ to hit the children.

2 The head teacher used to _____ the children whenever
   he could.

3 The Africans lived in poor conditions in poor areas called

   _____ .

4 Parents thought the Columbia Dance Hall would be bad or
   _____ for their children.

5 Ezekiel was angry and didn't want to _____ his
   employer anymore. He wanted to leave.

6 Ezekiel's mother developed a disease called _____ and
   couldn't control the sugar in her blood.

7 Ezekiel often did _____ , little jobs, for people at work.

8 At night there was a _____ . After this time, Africans
   weren't allowed to go out.

9 Ezekiel didn't like the way subjects were taught in schools and wanted
   to change the _____ .

10 The government thought that Ezekiel was a dangerous
   _____ who was trying to destroy the political system.

Word Focus

Complete the table with the missing words.

NOUN	ADJECTIVE	VERB
1 *debate*		debate
2 segregation		
3		compensate
4	divided	
5 witness		
6	insulted / ing	
7		dismiss
8	poor	
9		enforce
10	oppressive	
11 gossip		
12 commune		
13 (person)		represent
14		punish

Complete the sentences with one of the words from the table. You may need to change the form of the word.

1 Ma-Lebona was a ....*gossip*........ and liked to talk about other people.

2 Ezekiel used to meet with the men of the village around the
.... fire.

3 Ezekiel lost his job when he was .... from the school.

4 At St Peter's School, the students could talk about and ....
any subject they wanted.

5 Black and white people were .... and had to live separately.

6 Rebone was a .... to a murder. She saw her father kill the
policeman.

7 Dinku Dikae killed the policeman because he .... his family.

107

8 Coloured policemen were used to _____ the apartheid laws.

9 The Africans were very poor. This _____ often led to crime.

10 Africans didn't have a _____ in the government.

Useful Phrases

Choose the correct information to complete the sentences.

1 In Rebone, Ma-Lebona had met her (match) / suit.

2 Rebone wanted to take / scratch Ma-Lebona's eyes out.

3 The boys thought that Rebone had a face / cheek.

4 It was the dawn / sunrise of a new day.

5 The white people used phrases like 'put the kaffir in his seat / place'.

Match the lines above to the ones below.

a She behaved as if she were better than them and was arrogant. _3_

b She was her equal. _____

c This was offensive and intended to make Africans feel inferior. _____

d She wanted to hurt her. _____

e It was the start of a more positive time. _____

Grammar: *Be allowed to* and *have to*

Complete the sentences using the verbs in the box.

be allowed to	not be allowed to	have to	not have to

1 Coloured people _____*were allowed to*_____ travel by bus, but
   _____*had to*_____ sit in a corner on the top deck.

2 Black people _____ walk on the pavement
   with white people.

3 Often, Ezekiel _____ walk a long way to
   deliver washing.

4 Africans _____ make beer.

5 Ezekiel _____ go to the cinema.

6 Ezekiel _____ go into the white
   people's kitchen.

7 When King George V died, Ezekiel _____
   go to school.

8 On certain days, Ezekiel and his friends
   _____ go to the museum.

9 One time Ezekiel _____ stay on a bus
   and _____ walk a long way home.

10 White people _____ call Ezekiel by
   his name.

11 Ezekiel _____ use the stairs instead of
   the lift.

12 Africans _____ vote for black politicians
   in Parliament.

Grammar: Prepositions

Complete the sentences with a suitable preposition.

1 Ezekiel was interested __*in*__ literature.

2 His mother was extremely proud ＿＿＿＿ his success at school.

3 Ma-Lebona always complained ＿＿＿＿ her daughter-in-law.

4 Boeta Lem's father paid ＿＿＿＿ a lawyer when his son was arrested.

5 Aunt Dora always tried to deal ＿＿＿＿ her problems in the present.

6 The Africans were very afraid ＿＿＿＿ the police.

7 Ezekiel was jealous ＿＿＿＿ Rebone's boyfriend.

8 Ezekiel campaigned ＿＿＿＿ the Bantu Education Act.

9 He was sacked ＿＿＿＿ his teaching job.

10 He applied ＿＿＿＿ many other jobs in the following months.

Grammar: *Have something done*

Change the sentences using the structure *to have something done*.

1 Somebody did Mr Goldsmith's washing.

Mr Goldsmith had his washing done for him.

2 Someone brought Miss Forster alcohol from the shops.

3 Someone made clothes for the Afrikaners.

4 Someone built houses for the white men.

5 Someone made tea for all the office workers.

6 Servants did housework for white families.

7 In the pass office, someone took Ezekiel's photograph.

Published by Macmillan Heinemann ELT
Between Towns Road, Oxford OX4 3PP
A division of Macmillan Publishers Limited
Companies and representatives throughout the world
Heinemann is the registered trademark of Pearson Education, used under licence.

ISBN 978–0–2304–0867–8

This version of *Down Second Avenue* by Ezekiel Mphahlele was retold by
F H Cornish for Macmillan Readers.
First published 2011
Text © Macmillan Publishers Limited 2011
Design and illustration © Macmillan Publishers Limited 2011

Illustrated by Simon Williams
Cover photograph by Magnum Photos/Paolo Pellegrin.

Printed and bound in Thailand

2016   2015   2014   2013   2012   2011
10   9   8   7   6   5   4   3   2